THE
FUTURE WORLD
OF
ENERGY

Walt Disney World.
EPCOT CENTER BOOK

THE
FUTURE WORLD
OF
ENERGY

By John H. Douglas
and the Editors of Grolier

GROLIER

Grolier Incorporated
President and Chairman of the Board Robert B. Clarke

STAFF FOR THIS BOOK
Editor in Chief Kenneth W. Leish
Senior Editor Bernard M. Garfinkel
Art Director Don Longabucco
Picture Editors Laurie Platt Winfrey
Diane Raines Ward
Copy Editor Anne Glusker
Editorial Assistant Susan Stellingwerf
Production Manager Valerie Plue
Assistant Production Manager Margaret Fina
Consultant Victor K. McElheny, Director of Vannevar
Bush Fellowships, Massachusetts Insti-
tute of Technology

COVER: In the future, much of our oil will come from remote areas such as the North Sea's Brent field.

TITLE PAGE: Blazing in the desert sun at Barstow, California, 1,800 giant mirrors send solar rays to a tower where steam is produced; the steam powers a turbine that generates electricity. This is the world's largest solar power plant.

Library of Congress Cataloging in Publication Data

Douglas, John H., 1941-
  The future world of energy.

  (Walt Disney World EPCOT Center book)
  Includes index.
  Summary: Based on the Universe of Energy exhibit at Walt Disney's EPCOT Center, discusses the history and the future of energy
sources.
  1. Power resources—Juvenile literature. 2. Power resources—
Exhibitions—Florida—Juvenile literature. 3. EPCOT (Fla.)—Juvenile literature. [1. Power resources. 2. EPCOT (Fla.)] I. Grolier Incorporated. II. Title. III. Series.
TJ163.23.D68 1984   333.79   84-10886

ISBN 0-7172-8140-X

PICTURE CREDITS
The editors would like to express particular appreciation to Michael Melford and Wheeler Pictures for the creative photography at EPCOT Center and to Cooper/West/Nicholas Enterprises of London for the artwork that appears on pages 8–9, 12–13, 30, 75, 78, 87, 101, 105, 107–8. The illustrators include Tom Stimpson, Lionel Jeans, Andy Farmer, Mike Saunders, Chris Forsey, and Geoff Taylor. We would also like to thank Patrick Bunyan and Carolyn Raskin and the American Heritage Picture Library for their assistance. Cover & page 6: Co Rentmeester, courtesy of Exxon Corporation Pages 2 & 3: T. Zimberhoff/Sygma 4: Harvard Business School 10: Pacific Gas & Electric Chapter 2: Michael Melford, except for 16, 20, 22: Walt Disney Productions 26: Naval Research Lab 28: left, Sepp Seitz/Woodfin Camp; center, Claus Meyer/Black Star; right, Ken Sakamoto/Black Star 31 & 32: Granger Collection 33: General Motors 34: Metropolitan Museum of Art 36 & 37: New York Public Library 38: top, Science Museum, London; bottom, Peabody Museum, Salem, MA 40 & 42: Granger Collection 43: top, Mitchell Beazley Ltd. and Random House, Inc.; bottom, National Portrait Gallery, London 44: top, Granger Collection; bottom, Mabel Brady Garvan Collection, Yale University Art Gallery 46: S. B. Shiley/Bethlehem Steel p. 47: top, Library of Congress; bottom, Lewis Hine/George Eastman House 48 & 49: Library of Congress 50 & 51: John DeVisser/Black Star 52: University of Louisville, KY 53: American Petroleum Institute 54: Mitchell Beazley Ltd. and Random House, Inc. 55: Drake Well Museum 56: Theo R. Davis/Old Print Shop 58: Exxon 59: David Moore/Exxon 60: top, Robert Azzi/Woodfin Camp; bottom, R. J. Langlotz/Black Star 62: Jonathan Blair/Woodfin Camp 64: Exxon 65: NASA 66: General Dynamics 67: Mitchell Beazley Ltd. and Random House, Inc. 69: Society Library, NY 70: Dennis Brack/Black Star 71: John DeVisser/Black Star 72: Exxon 73: Los Alamos National Laboratory 76: Robert Michaels 80: Physics Today 81: top, Fritz Goro; bottom, H. Shaw Borst, Inc. 82: Department of Energy 84: Oak Ridge National Laboratory 86: Steve Smith/Wheeler Pictures 89: top, John McGrail/Wheeler Pictures; bottom, H. Shaw Borst Inc. 90: Chuck O'Rear/Woodfin Camp 93: top, Pierre Vauthy/Sygma; bottom, NASA 94: top, Solar Energy Research Institute; bottom, Dewitt Jones/Woodfin Camp 96: Department of Energy 97: Steve Northrup/Black Star 98 & 99: Tidal Power Corporation 100: James Balog/Black Star 102: NASA 104: Dan Budnik/Woodfin Camp 106: NASA

Contents

Chapter   Page

1. The New World of Energy 7

2. Exploring Universe of Energy 17

3. What Is Energy and Why Is It So Important? 27

4. From Campfire to Factory: The Continuing Search for Energy 35

5. The Age of Oil 51

6. The Energy Future: Fuels from the Earth 63

7. The Energy Future: Nuclear Power 79

8. The Energy Future: Sun, Wind, and Water 91

9. The Coming Energy Transition 103

    Glossary 110

    Index 111

Drilling for oil in Texas around 1930.

CHAPTER 1

The New World of Energy

The pale winter sun hits the northern coast of Maine. It is January 3, 2050, the first working day of the new year, and people in the northeastern corner of the United States are ready to resume their everyday activities after a long weekend of celebration.

The rising sun strikes the massive steel plates and girders of a giant offshore oil patform. This platform rides the stormy seas of the Atlantic, extracting oil from the ocean bottom more than a mile below the surface. Platforms such as this dot the remote ocean areas of the world, producing vital supplies of petroleum which are essential in maintaining a stable supply of energy. Global production of petroleum peaked in the first half of the century. But for some industries, and for most transportation purposes, oil is still the preferred fuel and still represents a sizable proportion of total energy use.

This huge energy facility represents a solid feat of twenty-first century technology. So too does the great tidal power station on the shore of the Bay of Fundy. Inside the station, massive generators produce a steady surge of electricity that flows to the cities, towns, and factories of New England.

At the half-century mark, Americans are enjoying an era of stable energy supply in which there is enough energy to meet the needs of a growing, highly technological society. But many older citizens remember the years of hard work and sacrifice that made today's abundance possible.

The Bay of Fundy power station is a case in point. Serious proposals had been made since the 1980s to use the bay's fifty-foot tides, the largest in the world, as a source of energy. In the 1980s, a much smaller tidal power station was constructed in a bay off the Bay of Fundy *(see Glossary, Tidal Energy)*. But it took billions of dollars

Symbolizing the constant search for new fuel supplies, the deep-sea platform Odin, off the Norwegian coast, will provide natural gas for the United Kingdom.

and years of negotiation between the United States and Canada before the great dam that now stretches between Maine and New Brunswick could be built. And the builders of the dam weighed every possible environmental impact.

Farther south, on Manhattan Island, a small plaque commemorates a legacy of the 1980s energy challenge. The plaque marks the spot where the first large fuel cell produced power for downtown New York City *(see Glossary, Fuel Cell)*. Now dozens of such cells meet the rising sun in gleaming array—twenty-foot-tall cylinders filled with hundreds of thin, disklike cells that are stacked like giant coins. The chemical reaction that takes place in these cells converts gas directly and efficiently into electricity, without the use of flame or the creation of pollution.

With breakfast over and New Year's resolutions more or less firmly in mind, millions of commuters along the eastern seaboard of the United States begin to go to work. For most, it is a brief, hassle-free trip. From Portland, Maine, to Miami, Florida, the East Coast cities of 2050 are spread out along transportation corridors. On either side of these corridors are easily accessible "open spaces"—natural, undeveloped areas. This trend began with the revolutionary changes brought about by computers. During the last ten years of the twentieth century, computers automated and decentralized industrial production. The result was a shift of the American economy toward white-collar work that could be done in small offices near workers' homes. These changes then fostered the development of new and efficient transportation systems. Railroad passengers travel on high-speed, magnetically levitated trains that connect nearby cities. These sleek vehicles ride silently and smoothly on a cushion of air. Commuters use local minibuses with computerized schedules that provide door-to-door service to their offices and back to their houses.

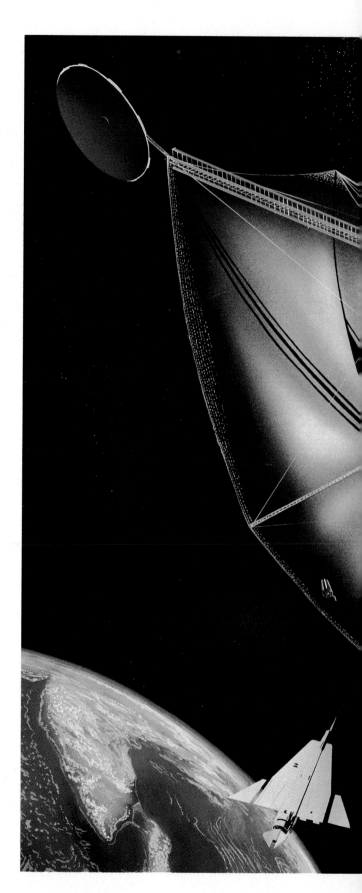

The space power station at right would convert solar energy into microwaves, which would be beamed to earth by giant transmitters at each end. On earth, the microwaves would be turned into electricity.

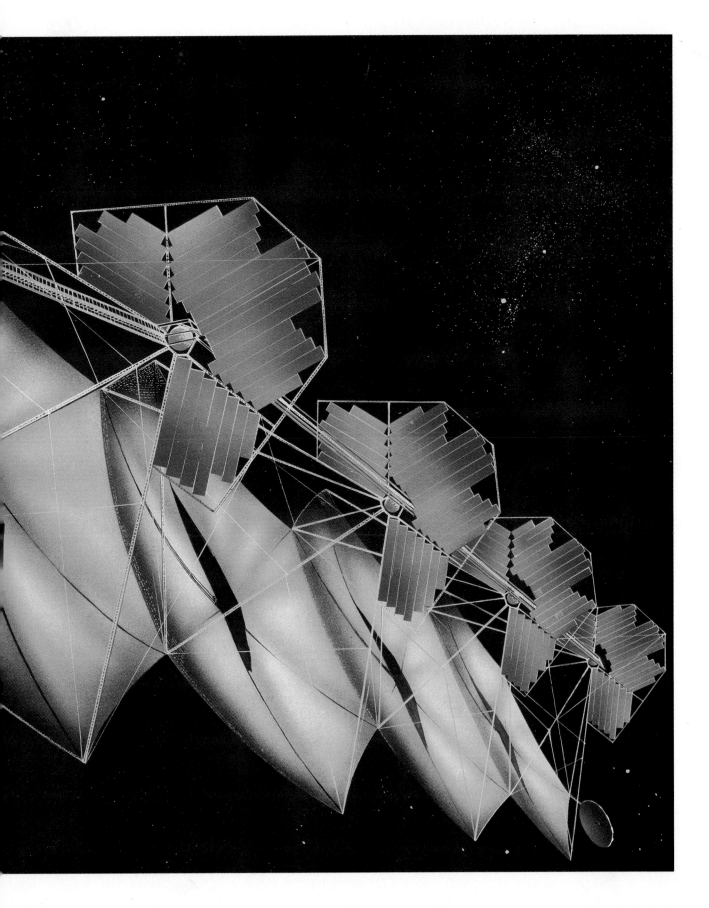

Using steam from 7,000 to 10,000 feet below ground, the geothermal energy complex at The Geysers in California provides power for a million homes.

Personal cars are still vital, of course—small electric vehicles for getting around town and highly efficient gasoline-powered automobiles for longer trips. But public transportation has become so reliable and convenient that many people now prefer to ride rather than drive to work.

The population of the United States is now nearly 350 million. This population growth has made the country increasingly conscious of the need to allow its cities to grow in ways that minimize pollution, reduce dependence on imported oil, and prevent destruction of farmland. As a result, substantial changes in patterns of living and commuting have taken place.

Inland from the mid-Atlantic coast, the sun rises over the Appalachian Mountains. This region is the source of much of the synthetic gas used in New York's fuel cells and of the electricity that runs America's new industries and transportation networks. Coal from seams buried within the mountains is transformed into more versatile liquid and gaseous fuels. In some areas, complex facilities that look something like old-fashioned oil refineries support the high-temperature chemical reactions that transform the coal. In others, the reactions take place in huge man-made caverns hundreds of feet below the earth's surface.

Each day, advanced power plants convert thousands of tons of Appalachian coal into electricity. This electricity is carried to urban areas by power lines with extremely high voltages. Such lines reduce the loss of electrical energy as it travels over long distances. This enables power plants to be built close to the coal mines. The arrangement has not only saved money but has also brought new industry into the region.

One of the clean and efficient new technologies used here to generate electricity from coal is fluidized bed combustion. In this process, crushed coal and limestone are burned to remove pollutants as they form. Gasification combined cycle plants are also used to generate electricity. In this process, coal is first transformed into a clean synthetic fuel and then burned in the same facility to generate electricity. The heat that is exchanged increases the efficiency of the operation.

Coal served as the vital "transition fuel." In this role, it brought the United States from the energy shortages of the late twentieth century to the stable abundance enjoyed in 2050. The other key source of that abundance is nuclear power, which now comes in two forms—fission and fusion (see Glossary). The sun is just rising in the Midwest, and there is no better place than Chicago to witness the importance of nuclear energy in 2050.

It was in this city in 1942 that the nuclear reactor was born. The first successful fission reaction took place in a crude facility that was built in a squash court at the University of Chicago's Stagg Field. By 1980, Chicago became one of the first large American cities to receive a major portion of its energy from nuclear power.

There were many temporary setbacks to the adoption of nuclear power. Among these were a slowdown in the demand for electricity in the late

1970s and the 1979 accident that shut down the nuclear reactor at Three Mile Island in Pennsylvania. Later in the century, utilities began to order reactors that were smaller and made use of new technologies. These reactors were tailored to the specific energy demands and financial requirements of localities.

Now, in 2050, Chicagoans are proud of their city's role in pioneering the use of these advanced reactors. The resulting efficient production of energy has been a major factor in fostering the city's growth. Chicago now receives power from three different types of nuclear reactors. One is a conventional fission reactor that is cooled by water. Another is a breeder reactor, which produces more fuel than it consumes (see Glossary, Nuclear Reactor). And the third is one of the new commercial fusion reactors, which produces energy by fusing together atoms of hydrogen rather than splitting atoms of uranium. It was the first put into operation in 2020.

Diversified Energy Production

As the sun moves westward, it reaches a region where it has become a major source of energy: the warm, dry southwestern quarter of the United States.

Here sunrise begins another day of solar-generated electric power and another cycle of solar heating and cooling (see Glossary, Solar Energy). Along a line from El Paso to Los Angeles, the southwestern district is dotted with solar energy facilities. They use hundreds of mirrors to track the sun and focus its light onto boilers on top of "power towers." The boilers are solar operated and create steam for generating electricity.

The roofs of most homes and many factories have some sort of flat-plate solar energy collector which produces hot water for heating, bathing, and industrial purposes. In rural areas, photovoltaic—or solar—cells convert sunlight into electricity for farms and ranches. The surplus power generated during the day is stored in batteries for use at night (see Glossary, Solar Cells).

In one particularly desolate area outside of Las Vegas, a small experimental facility presents a cluster of microwave antennas to the open sky.

These antennas receive power transmitted from a solar satellite whose orbit around the earth holds it stationary above this spot.

This microwave facility is a demonstration model designed to give scientists the opportunity to continue their research into this form of energy production. Research is currently proceeding on the design of larger satellites and improved antennas. Scientists are also investigating the environmental effects of microwave transmission.

Farther north, in Portland, Oregon, residents will not see the sun this morning. One of this area's frequent winter storms is lashing the coast. The fury of the storm is being put to good use, however, by the huge wind turbines that dot the coastal mountaintops. These turbines have rotor blades more than five hundred feet in diameter, and each can generate enough electricity to supply the energy needs of three thousand homes (see Glossary, Turbine).

North of San Francisco, a different form of energy is produced. Here, in an area known as The Geysers, natural eruptions of steam and hot water take place. This geothermal energy is used to generate electricity, as it has been for a period of more than ninety years (see Glossary, Geothermal Energy).

But during this time, many changes have taken place in the process. At first, only the "dry steam" erupting from the ground could be used to drive turbine generators. This meant that most of the heat energy contained beneath the surface was being wasted.

During the 1980s, engineers overcame the obstacles that had prevented the use of the subterranean hot water. One of these obstacles was the corrosive nature of the water. A second change took place in about 2010, when a process was developed to inject fresh water deep into the underlying layers of hot rock. This made it possible to tap the heat of these rocks directly.

Far across the Pacific, the first rays of the sun illuminate the islands of Hawaii. Here, floating in the water twenty-five miles from the island of Oahu, is one of the most technologically ambitious projects yet developed to harness renewable energy resources.

Called an ocean-thermal energy conversion (OTEC) system, this device pumps up cold Pacific Ocean water from great depths. The cold water is used to condense ammonia from a vapor into a liquid. Previously turned into vapor by using heat obtained from warm surface waters, the ammonia drives a turbine that generates electricity. In effect, the ammonia takes the place of steam in a steam turbine.

The great advantage of the ocean-thermal system is that the energy used to change liquid to gas and back again occurs naturally in ocean water. No fuel has to be burned.

Thinking About the Energy Future

Is this a forecast of the energy scene in the year 2050? Not really. No one can predict exactly what the mixture and abundance of the next century's energy sources will be. There are too many choices to be made and too many uncertainties in making them.

The precise nature of the future world of energy as we move into the twenty-first century will, of course, be determined by our response to the present energy challenge. That response will depend in large part on how well America's citizens understand today's energy problems and tomorrow's energy possibilities. The purpose of this book is to provide just such an understanding. Indecision about what should be done can delay vitally needed action and lead to serious energy shortages.

America's current energy problems and future energy possibilities have both been shaped by past experience in the development of energy re-

sources and technologies. It is not possible to explore the future world of energy without examining these past experiences in some detail.

At the same time, we must be aware of the exact nature of the energy challenge America now faces.

• About 70 percent of America's energy requirements are now supplied by oil and natural gas. Because of its unique advantages, oil will remain a vital source of energy for many decades to come. Easy to transport and store, oil is a highly concentrated and efficient source of energy. But the supply is limited. In the decades ahead, it will increasingly be used for purposes such as transportation, for which no other fuel functions as effectively. This will require the development and expansion of other sources of energy to augment the supply of petroleum.

At the same time, a shift in America toward electrification will result in an increased use of coal and nuclear power. Similarly, the growing use of electric heat pumps to heat and cool homes will result in a declining use of petroleum and natural gas for this purpose.

• The abundant supply of coal in the United States represents a vast store of available and relatively inexpensive energy. But without adequate safeguards, both mining coal and burning it can cause damage to the environment.

Mining coal once resulted in damage to local land and to water supplies. But surface reclamation and other measures aimed at protecting the environment are now established practices. The burning of coal, as with the combustion of other substances, releases pollutants into the atmosphere. For a number of years there has been a

Like the tip of an iceberg, only a small portion of this oceanic power station of the future is visible. Waters of different temperatures, from different depths, would be used in generating electrical power.

growing awareness that harmful pollution can and should be reduced or eliminated. Substantial progress has already been made in this area. Extensive research into newer technologies is also taking place, with further improvement expected in the future.

The costs of reclaiming land and preventing pollution, along with increasing transportation costs, have the effect of raising the price of coal. But coal's value to America as a source of energy is enormous.

Looking further into the future, scientists point to another cause for concern: the possibility that the burning of coal and other fossil fuels may cause a buildup of carbon dioxide in the atmosphere *(see Glossary, Fossil Fuels)*. This buildup might result in damaging climatic changes over a long period of time. Here again, extensive research is being done to explore the causes and effects of this potential threat to the environment.

• In the near future, the expansion of nuclear power in the U.S. will be limited to plants that are currently under construction. No new plants are being ordered.

There are two main reasons for this. One is that the growth in demand for electricity has been substantially lower than was expected in the 1970s, when a large number of plants were built and ordered. This decline in demand has led to a current excess of generating capacity.

The other reason is the high cost of new plants, caused by inflation and higher interest rates, along with political, social, and regulatory actions that have significantly extended construction times and costs.

The slowdown in construction of new nuclear plants creates a problem for the future, when increased generating capacity will be needed. The problem is compounded by public concern over nuclear safety.

Alternative reactor designs may offer additional safety features, but their use would require large

---

A nuclear fuel assembly rises out of a model of a reactor core at EPCOT Center's Energy Exchange. In an actual installation, each tube is filled with uranium pellets. The control rods are seen at right.

new investments and a renewed public acceptance of nuclear power.

As for the more distant future, fusion power would tap unlimited sources of energy in the form of hydrogen isotopes taken from sea water. (Isotopes are atoms of the same element that have different masses.) In addition, some scientists believe that fusion power will be safer than fission power. But scientists may never develop a workable fusion reactor.

• Renewable resources such as solar, geothermal, and wind energy have the potential to someday provide significant amounts of new energy. But in many cases the economic production of these resources will require the development of more efficient technologies.

Meanwhile, present technologies are helping renewable resources to find practical application. Many new homes, and some older ones, make use of passive solar heating, such as large windows that let the sun in. And despite their high cost, photovoltaic cells are gaining in popularity, particularly in remote areas not reached by electric power lines. The increasing use of solar heating and other renewable resources will reduce dependence on fossil fuels to some extent.

America's energy problems will also be affected by a number of trends and changes that are taking place in American life.

• More energy will be needed as the population of the U.S. continues to grow. Without increased amounts of energy, it will not be possible to maintain economic growth for this larger population. Conservation can reduce but not eliminate entirely the energy gap that will be created by America's population growth.

• Computers, robots, and various new industrial processes will encourage a long-established move toward electrification. At present, about one-third of all the energy used in the United States is converted to electricity. By the turn of the century, the proportion of energy converted to electricity should be close to 45 percent, and soon after it will rise to more than 50 percent. Since electricity can be produced by using various sources of energy, from coal to wind power, this trend will lessen our dependence on petroleum.

• Water is needed to develop synthetic fuels. Lack of adequate water resources, especially in the western United States, may diminish the huge production potential of these new fuels.

• In the years ahead, agriculture may require more energy. One reason is a trend toward the use of mechanized equipment. In addition, some farmland will be lost to urban growth. More marginal land may then have to be devoted to agriculture. New technologies will be needed to grow more crops on less acreage and on less fertile land, and these technologies will use more energy.

• Energy will cost more to produce. The protection of the environment will remain an important concern. At the same time, the growth in population and in the economy will strain our land, water, and air resources. The goals of preventing pollution and conserving natural resources will raise the cost of producing energy.

Meeting the Challenge

Only time will tell whether America can succeed in solving its energy problems. What we do know is that the challenge is here now, and it requires two major, parallel courses of action. One is to develop our resources of oil and natural gas and to use them carefully in the future. The second is to develop alternative sources of energy.

The U.S. must lead the way in meeting this challenge. Because of its size and its particular path of development, America has always been a major consumer of energy. Even with conservation and other limits on the use of energy, America must still develop new energy sources.

The challenge is so great that it may well result in one of the world's most creative and productive periods, an era that is marked by new ideas, new explorations, a new burst of technological innovation.

Poised on the brink of a new energy age, we can begin by facing an inescapable fact. The amount of energy we will have available in our future society will largely shape our acts and days, largely control our economic and social activities. Can we do it? In the pages ahead, we will try to answer that question, as we explore the past, present, and future world of energy.

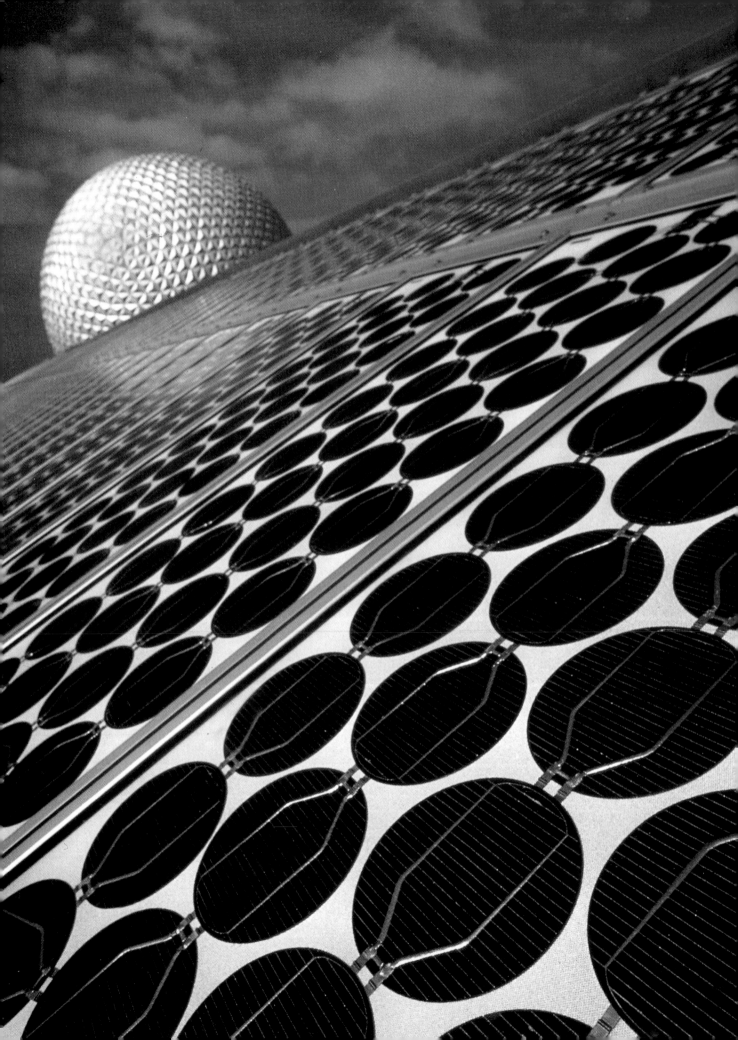

CHAPTER 2

Exploring Universe of Energy

Shining in the brilliant Florida sun, its polished walls glowing with color, "Universe of Energy" at EPCOT Center seems to radiate power. In fact, an important function of the building is to absorb energy from the sun and put it to work. An array of 2,200 solar panels covers the sloping roof of the diamond-shaped structure, making it the largest privately funded solar-power installation in the world. Approximately 80,000 photovoltaic cells in the panels convert sunlight directly into electricity. Inside, a dozen conveyances called "traveling theater" cars use this power to carry visitors through the exhibit's energy-related adventures, which range from giant-screen movies to an encounter with a herd of life-size dinosaurs.

Like its gleaming exterior, Universe of Energy, presented by Exxon Corporation, is designed to dramatize the important role energy plays in our lives. The exhibit turns abstract ideas about energy into direct personal experiences. Visitors smell the odor of a primeval swamp. They witness the toil of those involved in searching for new sources of fuel. They wonder at the promise of a future world of energy.

Universe of Energy was created to interpret the past, present, and future world of energy for an audience of all ages. In a series of dramatic and entertaining experiences, the exhibit advances new energy ideas and technologies and explains basic energy concepts. It illustrates current sources of energy and underlines the effort that will be required to meet future energy needs.

A journey into Universe of Energy begins with a unique vision of energy as art. In the preshow waiting area, multiple images dance across one hundred movable sections of a huge screen, revealing the complex nature and fascinating variety of energy in all its forms. Each rotating section has three surfaces—one black, the other two white for image projection. Five projectors cast

Atop Universe of Energy at EPCOT Center are 80,000 photovoltaic cells (left). They convert solar energy into electricity to help power the "traveling theater" cars that transport visitors during the show.

Exxon Corporation's Universe of Energy is one of the most popular attractions at EPCOT Center.

rapidly changing pictures onto the screen, timed to coincide with the changing surfaces. The effect is to create a three-dimensional kaleidoscope of images and information about energy.

From this living mosaic the visitor begins to perceive, almost subconsciously, the theme that will be repeated in various ways throughout the rest of the exhibit. Energy is all around us, a vital but often unappreciated part of daily life and a reality that can no longer be taken for granted.

The many faces of energy dance across the huge screen. We see images of heat, light, electricity, chemical reactions, and nuclear power. Their constant change and interplay illustrate a fundamental lesson about the nature of energy— that it is neither created nor destroyed, but only transformed.

Humans appear—harnessing fire, sailing before the wind, using the power of falling water to run their mills. These three forms of energy—fire, wind, and water—helped sustain the great civilizations of the past. They provided domestic heat, wind power for ocean trade, and mechanical power for grinding meal.

With the Industrial Revolution came a fundamental shift in energy use, as coal became the ideal fuel to run steam engines. Then, in less than a century, the world became highly dependent on oil. The preshow program ends with a reminder that resources of oil and natural gas are limited

and that the search for new forms of energy is one of the most important challenges now facing mankind.

The Primeval World of Energy

The musical theme song, "Energy, You Make the World Go 'Round," rises in the background, and visitors enter what appears to be a conventional theater. But then the lights dim and the entire theater floor seems to float. The audience is actually seated in "traveling theater" cars, each holding up to 98 passengers. The cars are lifted on a giant turntable that floats on a thin cushion of air as it rotates. Now the audience faces a huge screen, 155 feet wide and nearly three stories high. The audience is about to see the largest animated film ever made, a truly epic motion picture that describes how the earth's primary energy resources—fossil fuels—were created more than a billion years ago.

A lush, primeval landscape flashes on the screen. Lightning shatters the sky, releasing energy into the atmosphere. This energy sparks the complex chemical reactions that form organic molecules and eventually lead to the emergence of life. Sunlight falls upon the sea, where it is absorbed by microscopic plants. These in turn are eaten by tiny animals. As the animals die and settle to the ocean floor, they are trapped in layers of sediment. Transformed by millions of years of heat, pressure, and the action of bacteria, this trapped organic material becomes oil and gas.

On land a similar process takes place, but on a grander scale. Here roam the dinosaurs, lords of a damp world filled with swamps and forests of giant, fernlike trees. Through photosynthesis and the food chain, these plants and animals convert the energy of sunlight into the chemical energy of organic molecules that they need in order to live and grow (*see Glossary, Photosynthesis*). When they die, they quickly decay and form a soft, rich organic mass called peat. This organic mass is trapped under layers of mud and sand, compressing the soft peat until it hardens into coal.

Suddenly, the last images of ancient life and death fade, and the six "traveling theater" cars turn and move forward in formation, traveling out of the theater into an amazingly lifelike re-creation of the young earth the audience has just seen on film.

A giant creature with many legs—a millipede—looms among ferns grown far beyond their familiar size. This is a world that dwarfs the human scale. A musky odor arises from the surrounding swamp. It is the symbol and the symptom of the process of decay that transforms lush plant growth and living animals into deposits of fossil fuel.

Just ahead a brontosaurus feeds in a stagnant pool. He seems fearsomely alive—his long, powerful neck towering high above the slowly moving theater cars. Water drips from his mouth as he munches away like a monstrous cow chewing her cud. The brontosaurus seems peaceful enough, but this was also an age when the largest meat eaters of all time roamed the land.

Now the cars move ahead one by one, and the ferocity of life at this time is soon confirmed by a growl from one of these mighty hunters. On the riverbank an allosaurus rears on its hind legs to

Images of energy through the ages are projected on a giant screen with 100 movable sections at the preshow at Universe of Energy (below).

attack a heavily armored stegosaurus, which defends itself with powerful strokes of its spiked tail. (Audio-Animatronics creations that breathe, growl, and fight, these dinosaurs are the largest animated creatures ever fabricated. They hold center stage against a 515-foot scenic background that took 6,000 man-hours to paint.)

But the size and might of these animals is no match for the powerful forces of the still-restless earth. An earthquake rumbles across the darkening landscape, shifting the ground and trapping three dinosaurs in a mud pit. Then the most awesome of all nature's giants, an erupting volcano, begins to spit molten lava. The air is filled with the harsh smell of sulfur. With a roar, the volcano seems to draw the audience into its fiery center.

The Present Energy Challenge

Darkness descends. The cars travel through a mist and the scene shifts. We move from the struggles of dinosaurs in a primitive world to a present-day challenge that, in its own way, is just as awesome. Emerging into the twentieth century, the "traveling theater" cars reassemble before a 210-foot-wide wraparound screen in the main theater. Here, in a live-action film, the ongoing search for new sources of energy is presented in a quick succession of dramatic scenes. Hundreds of mir-

Today's fossil fuels can be traced back to the Mesozoic era, which is recreated at EPCOT's Universe of Energy. Below, towering brontosaurs graze.

rors gleam in tranquil splendor at a solar-energy facility in the California desert. A howling, icy wind hampers efforts to drill for oil from a platform in the stormy North Sea. In the silent darkness of outer space, a satellite records images of the earth's terrain that may reveal undiscovered deposits of fossil fuel.

For all its spectacular pictures of gigantic equipment and fearful landscapes, the film also shows that the search for energy is a highly personal drama. In a quiet laboratory, scientists carry out the complex search for new oil as they "read" a confusing jumble of graphs that record vibrations in the earth. Underground miners, dwarfed by their digging machines, cut rock-hard coal from its ancient bed. On a deep-sea drilling platform far out in rolling ocean seas, oil workers muscle drilling pipes around the slippery floor in a breathtaking demonstration of split-second timing.

The world's varied energy resources flash by in quick, sharp images. Picturesque Dutch windmills with wooden arms covered by cloth sails contrast with sleek new wind turbines for generating electricity. One of the largest operating breeder reactors, Phénix, stands out among the wine vineyards of southern France. Tar sands in the rugged terrain of the Canadian wilderness yield up their sticky black treasure. Beginning at the North Slope oil fields high in the Arctic, the Trans-Alaska Pipeline spans 800 miles of sometimes barren wasteland—now buried deep in snowdrifts, now dipping toward its final destination at the Alaskan port of Valdez. Dotted across the vast Saudi Arabian desert stretch the producing wells that tap the world's richest petroleum basin. A complicated Tokamak apparatus dominates the center of a cluttered laboratory building (*see Glossary, Tokamak*). The Tokamak heats and confines hydrogen isotopes as scientists probe for the secrets of fusion energy.

Varied as they are, these images convey a clear message. The quest for energy is becoming ever more difficult, challenging both the imagination and the stamina of those who seek to develop new resources. Instead of relying on just one primary fuel, such as oil, for future energy growth, the world will have to develop alternatives that range

A meat-eating allosaurus battles a stegosaur (top), which uses its deadly spiked tail as a weapon. Above, a placid edaphosaurus peers out of the foliage at Universe of Energy visitors.

from solar power to nuclear fusion. Conservation of the remaining supply of oil is vitally important. Through the use of cars that are more fuel efficient, better insulation of homes, and the development of other fuels, conservation will play an integral part in guaranteeing that future generations have enough energy.

The passengers in the "traveling theater" cars return to the triangular room where they began their fascinating journey. Many may not be aware that these cars are the largest electric vehicles of their kind ever built. Each weighs more than fifteen tons when fully loaded, yet each is driven by a single six-horsepower electric motor powered by eight storage batteries. The cars recharge while they are stationary. The batteries don't have to be "plugged in" for this recharging. Electrical energy, produced in part by the rooftop solar panels, radiates across the thin airspace between the floor and the cars. A thin wire embedded in the concrete floor guides the cars by communicating start, stop, and turn instructions.

Now the curtains that cover the side walls are raised to reveal a huge mirrored surface. The illusion is startling. It's like sitting in a reflecting circle the size of a football field. The audience is surrounded by images created by a computer and projected in dazzling, laserlike light.

The images again relate energy to daily life. Energy is seen as the driving force behind the most diverse activities, from transportation and agriculture to communications and recreation. The audience hears a message calling for cooperation

In these scenes from the Universe of Energy film, a worker (above) connects drilling pipes on an offshore oil platform (below). Such platforms, which can cost more to build than a skyscraper, play a key role in the worldwide search for new supplies of oil.

among industry, the government, and the public if these scenes of prosperity are to continue. The final image appears. It is a reminder of the human impact of energy on modern life. A stream of computerized laser drawings shows a little girl growing up in a time of energy abundance to become an astronaut who will challenge the future in space.

Learning About Energy

The EPCOT Center energy story continues at Exxon Corporation's "Energy Exchange." Located in CommuniCore, this try-it-yourself demonstration gives visitors the opportunity to explore the wonders and mysteries of energy firsthand. Here, too, they can learn more about some of the energy sources featured in Universe of Energy.

The open, spacious demonstration area is dominated by a large model of a deep-sea drilling platform. Nearly as impressive are a sixteen-ton chunk of Colorado oil shale and the giant bucket from a power shovel similar to those used to extract coal from surface mines. These and other examples of energy sources and technology are laid out to see, touch, and even play with.

The operative approach is that learning can be fun. Play is, in fact, a particularly effective way to convey knowledge about a subject as complex as energy. How much energy can be produced by a person pedaling on a bicycle, and what does this energy mean in your life? You discover that pedaling steadily for seven days produces the same amount of energy as is contained in one gallon of gasoline. (It's brisk exercise.)

Such play puts the cost of energy into exact perspective. At another demonstration, you can turn a crank to make a hundred-watt bulb glow brightly. You then discover that it would take a week of turning at this rate to generate one dollar's worth of electricity.

The demonstration area also has scale models of energy facilities and pieces of equipment that are used in these facilities. These too provide a unique opportunity to inspect at close range some of the energy technology that plays an important role in daily life, but that few people outside the industry ever see. There is a simulated nuclear-

In Energy Exchange (above), visitors see some of the equipment used to drill for oil. Below are a mill tooth bit (1), used for chipping away rock; a tungsten carbide insert bit (2), which crushes rock as it rotates; a diamond bit (3), used on the hardest rocks; and a polycrystalline bit (4).

The 30,000-pound piece of oil shale above contains enough oil to provide fuel for a car for one year.

In Energy Exchange, a couple stops photovoltaic cells from rotating by placing their hands between the cells and the light (above). The girl below is learning how much pedaling it takes to produce as much energy as a gallon of gas: seven days' worth.

reactor core, holding control rods that visitors can manipulate. There is a blowout-preventer from an oil well, along with an explanation of how it works to prevent spectacular but wasteful "gushers." There are examples of different kinds of deep-sea drilling platforms, reconstructed in incredible detail. These provide immediate insight into the difficulties of oil production in hostile seas.

And for those with specific questions, a bank of computer terminals with "touch-a-screen" communication provides answers. Questions selected from a multiple-choice format are answered with short television presentations that make use of the latest videodisc technology. Ask how coal is produced, for example, and you will see a brief but informative movie of men at work in an underground mine. Ask about energy demand, and you will be presented with specific facts and figures. It is startling to learn, for instance, that the energy used each day in the United States is equivalent to burning seven gallons of oil for every man, woman, and child in the country.

For more than a century, great exhibitions in America have provided a good way for the general public to learn more about new science, art, technology, and life-styles. These exhibitions have, in fact, been useful in helping to introduce and explain new technologies. The first major demonstration of the telephone took place at the Centennial Exposition in Philadelphia in 1876. The marvels of electricity were featured at the World's Columbian Exposition in Chicago in 1893.

In this tradition, Universe of Energy and Energy Exchange at EPCOT Center present the story of energy in a uniquely entertaining and informative way—and at a highly appropriate time. We must now try to understand our energy problems in order to solve them. Yet most people have little opportunity to explore the intricacies of energy firsthand. Exxon Corporation's energy exhibits neatly fill this gap.

The display at right shows where the world's coal reserves are located. Each color represents a country; the United States (blue) has 25% of the world's coal.

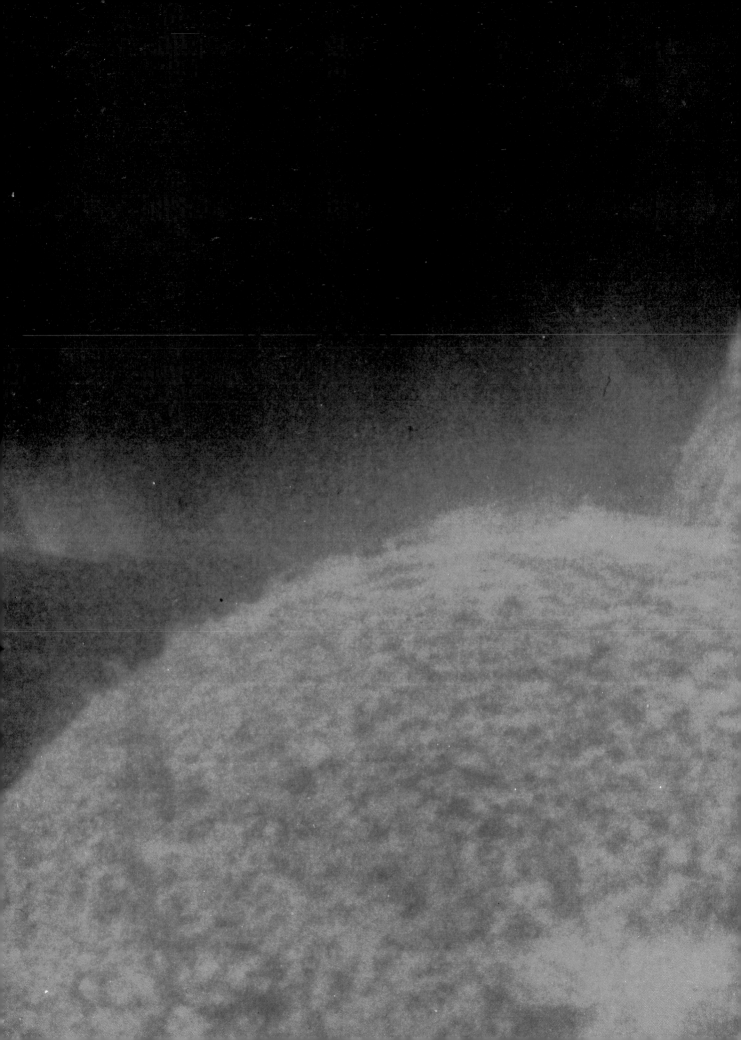

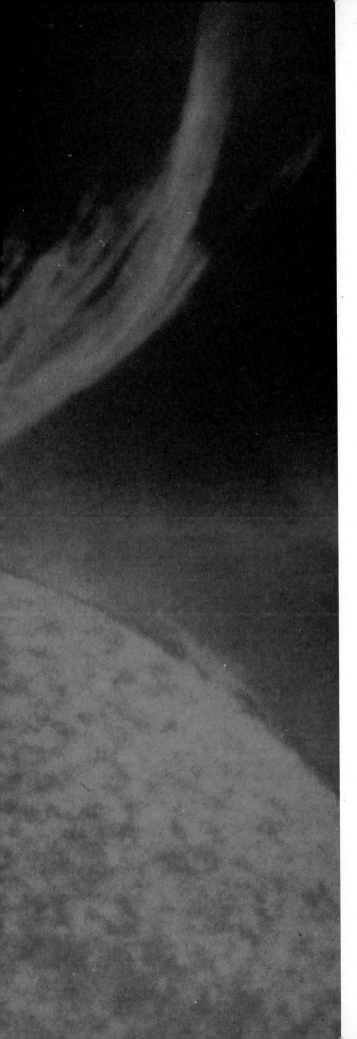

CHAPTER 3

What Is Energy and Why Is It So Important?

Energy is all around us, but few people understand exactly where it comes from and what it does. Ancient peoples were awed by the power of the sun to illuminate their world and warm their bodies. But they had little if any knowledge of how this distant source produced these effects. Heat and light are two of the most common forms of energy. Yet for thousands of years scientists did not completely understand the relationship between them. It was only in the nineteenth century that an explanation of this relationship began to emerge. And a scientific account of precisely how the sun produces energy was not formulated until the 1930s.

Even today, with all of our recently acquired knowledge, we may not be aware that much of the energy used in daily life originates from the sun's heat and light. All green plants depend on sunlight to drive the complex chemical reactions involved in photosynthesis. These reactions produce carbohydrate molecules that allow the plants to live and grow. Animals and people in turn eat the plants. They use the chemical energy stored in carbohydrates to make the proteins that are necessary for their own life and growth. (Biologists call this the food chain.) A man lifting an iron bar is thus, indirectly, using up solar energy.

The sun produces useful energy in numerous other ways. Heat from the sun evaporates moisture from the sea. The moisture eventually falls as rain upon the land. As this water runs downhill toward the sea, the energy of its motion can be captured by a turbine to generate electricity. Thus hydroelectric power is also a form of solar energy. So is the motion of a sailboat or a kite. Wind, too,

A giant eruption leaps from the sun's surface in this photograph taken on August 21, 1973. Most of the energy we use originates from the sun's heat and light.

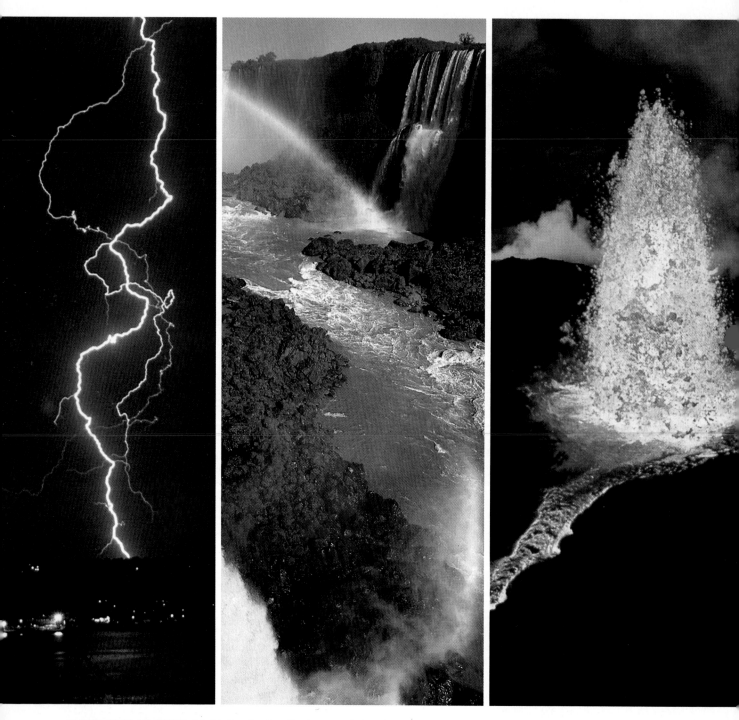

ENERGY IN NATURE: Lightning is the discharge of electric energy from clouds. Falling water is a powerful source of mechanical energy. A volcano gives off intense heat energy.

is produced by the motion of air—which begins to rise when it absorbs the heat of the sun.

Fossil fuels represent a particularly useful form of "captured sunshine." In oil, coal, and natural gas, the carbon and hydrogen atoms that once made up the molecules of living tissue are now available for burning. The sun's energy caused the formation of this organic material millions of years ago, through photosynthesis. Burial deep in the earth preserved the molecules and transformed them into their present form. Burning releases this stored chemical energy as heat. This heat can be further converted into mechanical energy to do work, that is, to make something move. An automobile engine, for example, uses the expansion of hot gases from burning fuel to push pistons and drive the wheels of an automobile.

Trying to understand the connections among various forms of energy has fascinated some of the world's greatest thinkers for centuries, often in surprisingly personal ways. Albert Einstein devoted his life to probing the theoretical relationship between energy and matter. When away from his calculations he would spend countless hours sailing in a small boat, observing the energetic play of wind and waves. His wife once admitted that Einstein never learned to drive a car because it was "too complicated" for him. But he felt a deep and natural response to the play of forces involved in sailing and experienced what one friend described as a "childlike delight" when his boat was suddenly becalmed.

Over the centuries, it has taken just that kind of attentive, sometimes playful observation by scientists to uncover the secrets of energy. Michael Faraday was an English scientist who explained the vital connection between electricity and magnetism. Faraday took so much pleasure in his work that every Christmas he shared his discoveries with groups of children, explaining to them the mysteries of his experiments.

The Transformation of Energy

Many of the early scientists who devoted their lives to studying energy had one main objective. They wanted to learn the conditions that governed the transformation of one form of energy into an-

other. These rules were finally established during the first half of the nineteenth century, and they form the basis of the science of thermodynamics, the science concerned with the nature of heat and how it is converted into other forms of energy—such as mechanical energy—to do work (*see Glossary, Thermodynamics*).

Probably the best way to understand the problem of energy transformation is to consider a modern example. When gasoline is burned in an automobile engine, energy is released as heat. Some of this heat causes the gases inside a cylinder to expand and drive a piston. Some is lost in the exhaust. The mechanical energy of the engine performs work by moving the car. But, again, some energy is lost through friction between the wheels and the highway.

This process raises two questions. One is: does any of the energy actually disappear? The other is: can *all* of the heat be converted into useful work? In answering these two questions, scientists formulated the first and second laws of thermodynamics. It is these laws which, ever since their discovery, have guided and shaped the continuing effort to design more efficient engines.

Until the late 1700s, heat was thought to be a fluid called "caloric." It supposedly flowed out of hot objects and into cold ones. This theory originated with the ancient Greek philosophers. It was finally disproved by Benjamin Thompson (later Count Rumford) around 1798. Born in America, Rumford sided with the British during the Revolutionary War and spent the rest of his life in Europe. During service as minister of war and police in Bavaria, he watched the barrel of a cannon being drilled out. He noticed that the amount of heat released during the drilling depended only on the energy involved in turning the drill. It did not depend on the quantity of metal that was removed. This, he knew, did not fit in with the idea that heat was a fluid contained in the metal and released when the drill cut into it.

Rumford set up a crude experiment to explore this puzzle. In the experiment, Rumford brought eighteen pounds of water to a boil in two hours and forty-five minutes solely through the heat of friction. He created the friction by having a piece

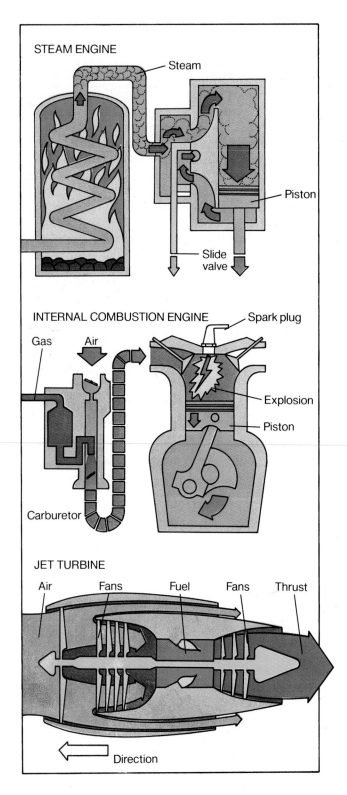

STEAM ENGINE

Steam

Piston

Slide valve

INTERNAL COMBUSTION ENGINE

Spark plug

Gas

Air

Explosion

Piston

Carburetor

JET TURBINE

Air Fans Fuel Fans Thrust

Direction

of steel rub against a rotating cylinder of metal. Onlookers were astonished at the amount of heat produced by Rumford's ingenious apparatus. But much more careful measurements would be required to determine the precise quantity of heat produced by a precise amount of work.

During the 1840s, the British physicist James Joule finally conducted the critical experiments that measured the exact relationship between heat and mechanical energy. Joule constructed a cylindrical vessel in which water could be stirred. Then he rotated paddles through the water and measured the temperature change. The work applied in rotating the paddles could be measured. This work, in turn, produced a precise amount of heat, which could also be measured.

One common unit for measuring work is the "foot-pound." If you lift a one-pound weight one foot off the ground, you have done one foot-pound of work. Because of Joule's experiments, we now know it takes 778 foot-pounds of work to raise the temperature of one pound of water by one degree Fahrenheit. The heat thus produced is called the British Thermal Unit, or BTU.

In the metric system, the unit for measuring heat is the "calorie" (*see Glossary*). The unit for work and energy is the "joule," in honor of James Joule (*see Glossary*). It takes 4.186 joules of work to produce one calorie of heat. (One BTU represents about the same quantity of heat as 250 calories.)

The final answer to the question about whether energy is ever really "lost" came in 1847. In that year, a German physicist, Hermann von Helmholtz, published the scientific paper that firmly established heat as another form of energy, not a separate kind of matter. Von Helmholtz also stated

Three kinds of engines that convert hot expanding gases into mechanical energy are shown at left. In the steam engine, top, water is boiled and the resulting steam is directed by a slide valve to push a piston in one direction or the other. In the internal combustion engine, center, the piston is pushed by the explosion of gasoline mixed with air. The jet engine, bottom, has fans that compress incoming air that is burned with fuel to provide thrust.

the first law of thermodynamics in more or less its present form: *energy can neither be created nor destroyed.* When energy seems to disappear, it is actually being given off as heat.

The conversion of heat to mechanical energy, in fact, provides many of the benefits of modern life. Heat is converted into mechanical energy by using an engine. The mechanical energy the engine produces is then used to perform work. Usually, heat is made to produce mechanical energy by heating a gas and causing it to expand. In a steam engine, for example, water is boiled. The expanding steam passes through a valve into a cylinder, where it pushes a piston. The moving piston creates mechanical energy. In an automobile engine, a mixture of gasoline and air is ignited inside the cylinder. This causes a small explosion that moves the piston and produces mechanical energy. In a turbine or jet engine, hot burning gases push past blades set into a shaft. The expanding gases cause the shaft to rotate like a pinwheel in a breeze, producing mechanical energy.

The second important question scientists asked about energy during the first half of the nineteenth century was whether this conversion of heat into mechanical energy could ever be complete. The short answer is no—there is always some waste involved. A more formal answer was set forth as the second law of thermodynamics in 1824 by Nicolas Carnot, a French physicist who was trying to improve the efficiency of the steam engine.

Carnot did not conduct exhaustive experiments on different kinds of engines. Instead, he published a theoretical essay, "Reflections," about how engines work. In simple terms, his theory went like this: the hotter a gas is, the greater pressure it can exert on a piston. Similarly, the cooler the gas becomes after its expansion, the faster the piston will return to its starting point. The reason for this is that the cooler gas exerts less pressure to keep the piston up. There is no way, however, to remove all the heat from the gas. So some of the heat energy will always be wasted.

Carnot therefore concluded that only a fraction of the heat used to run an engine actually shows up as useful work. This fraction, expressed as a percent, is called the "efficiency" of an engine.

The first electric motor (top) was invented in 1831 by Joseph Henry, above. An iron rod wrapped with wire rocked on a pivot; the wires alternately touched electricity-producing cells on each end and created magnetic fields that reversed the motion of the rod.

The most efficient engines have the greatest differences between the initial (hot) temperature of the gas and the final (cool) temperature of the gas inside the engine. The greater the difference in temperature, the greater the transformation of heat into mechanical energy. But this transformation can never be complete. An engine with 100 percent efficiency would be a perpetual-motion machine. According to the second law of thermodynamics, such a machine is impossible to create.

Most engines have fairly low efficiencies. Steam engines with pistons, for example, have efficiencies that range from 5 percent to 15 percent. The difference depends on the initial temperature of the steam. Burning gasoline produces gases that are much hotter than steam, so an automobile engine has an efficiency of about 25 percent. Tur-

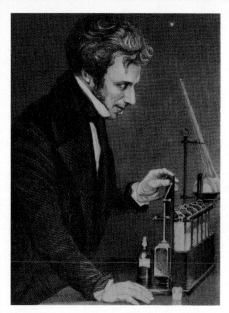

New Insights Into Electricity

Michael Faraday, the English chemist and physicist, discovered that a magnet moving through a coil of wire would make electricity flow inside the wire. Joseph Henry made the same discovery in America at about the same time. The importance of their work was to provide a more practical way to generate electricity. Previously, electric currents had been produced by battery cells, which could produce only small amounts of energy. Based on the work of Faraday and Henry, however, engineers learned how to build generators in which electricity was created by spinning a magnet inside a coil of wire. The magnet could be turned by any convenient source of mechanical energy—steam, water, even a hand crank. Faraday also discovered chemical properties of atoms that provided the first hint of the existence of electrons, the charges that make up electricity.

bines have efficiencies approaching 40 percent. The temperature of a gas in a turbine drops further after it passes over many blades on a rotating shaft than it does after passing once through the cylinder of a piston engine.

Electricity as a Source of Energy

Steam and gasoline engines convert heat directly into mechanical energy. Electricity provides an indirect way of converting heat into mechanical energy. In a power plant, fuels provide the heat energy that spins a turbine. The turbine drives a generator that generates electricity. The electricity, in turn, is used to run an engine that produces mechanical energy.

Until modern times, electricity remained one of the most mysterious phenomena in nature (*see Glossary, Electricity*). Around 600 B.C., the Greek philosopher Thales of Miletus performed some of the first simple experiments involving electricity. Thales rubbed a piece of amber with a cloth. This created an electric charge on the amber. The charge was evident because the amber then attracted bits of feathers and pith (the material inside a plant stem). Thales did not realize that he had produced the same sort of electric charge that is contained in the lightning that goes crashing through the sky. Only later did scientists discover that the charge on the amber consisted of electrons and that these electrons could be made to flow down a wire as an electric current. After Thales's experiments, little more was learned about electricity for almost a thousand years.

Then, in 1600, an English physician named William Gilbert published a book explaining his experiments, which were much like those of Thales. Sixty years later, a German physicist, Otto von Guericke, built a crank-driven machine that could produce larger amounts of an electric charge than was possible by rubbing amber.

This invention made it easier for scientists to study the behavior of electric charges. But progress toward the discovery of electric currents remained slow. The capacity of metals to conduct electricity wasn't discovered for another forty years. The invention of a reliable way to produce an electric current using a battery did not occur until one hundred years later, about 1800. Then, in 1831, two men working independently discovered the principle that made possible the invention of electrical generators and motors. The English physicist and chemist Michael Faraday and the American physicist Joseph Henry found that a magnet moving through a coil of wire would make electricity flow through the wire. This meant that almost any source of mechanical energy—from falling water to a steam engine—could be used to generate electricity by spinning a magnet inside a coil. Conversely, sending a current through a coil of wire that is inside a magnetic field will make the coil turn. This principle is the basis of electric motors, which use electrical energy to create mechanical energy.

Most electricity today is generated in steam-turbine power plants. Heat from burning coal or fuel oil, or from a nuclear reactor, creates steam that is "superheated" at high pressure to more than 1,000 degrees Fahrenheit. As it passes through the turbine, the steam is cooled to less than 100 degrees Fahrenheit. This produces a highly efficient transfer of energy. One turbine-driven generator can supply the electric power needed by about 500,000 homes.

Electrical energy is usually measured in kilowatt-hours (KWh). One KWh equals exactly 3.6 million joules of energy. An average residence uses about 660 kilowatt-hours of electricity each month. Approximately one-third of all the energy used each year in the United States goes to generate electricity.

Industry in America is the largest user of electricity. But residential use almost equals industrial use. When residential use is combined with commercial use, the total exceeds industrial consumption. Generally, residential/commercial use of electricity is for heating, lighting, and appliances. Industrial use includes these things plus the electricity used to run heavy equipment.

Electrical generators and appliances are rated by their power—that is, the amount of energy they produce or consume each second. A commonly used unit of power is the kilowatt, which is equal to the consumption of one thousand joules of energy per second.

Increasing automation, exemplified by the robot arms welding a car above, depends on electric power, the most versatile form of energy.

Major coal and nuclear power plants can generate electricity at the rate of one million kilowatts, or one billion joules per second.

National Energy Needs

In speaking of national energy needs, it is no longer meaningful to talk in terms of individual BTUs of heat or joules of work. Instead, the unit commonly used to describe national energy supplies is the "quad." This stands for one quadrillion BTUs (a quadrillion is a one followed by fifteen zeros). Using energy at the rate of one quad per year roughly equals burning half a million barrels of oil every day for a year. In 1981, the United States consumed 74.7 quads of energy in all its commercially available forms.

Obviously, for economic expansion to keep up with population growth, more energy will be needed. Just to accommodate an expanding American work force, a steady increase in the growth of energy in the United States will be required. This increase has been calculated to be at least 1.5 percent per year through the turn of the century. This increase includes a 3.3 percent annual growth rate for electricity. In short, America and the world face a dilemma: it will be necessary to produce vast amounts of new energy at the same time that the supply of petroleum, a current major source of energy, is declining.

During the course of human history, man has managed to find new sources of energy when the forces of progress and change demanded them. Is the present energy challenge so different from those of the past? To answer that question, we must take a look at earlier energy times.

33

CHAPTER 4

From Campfire to Factory: The Continuing Search for Energy

The search for energy sources began with the discovery of fire by early humans who were trying to survive in a hostile environment. It has continued ever since as a vital part of the quest to improve the human condition.

Over the years, this search went hand in hand with history's greatest discoveries and innovations. The wheel, the plow, sailing ships, and steam engines, among many other advances, extended the human capacity to do work using new sources of energy. Advances like these also created social changes, such as the Industrial Revolution. These changes, in turn, stimulated further energy exploration.

The search for new and larger sources of energy has also created periodic fuel shortages and environmental damage. To provide wood for fuel and lumber, early civilizations used up great forests that once covered much of the Middle East. Burning fuel also damaged the environment. Air pollution in larger cities and towns was already a serious problem in the Middle Ages.

Over the last 200 years, the pace of energy change has accelerated dramatically. Per capita energy use in the United States has risen roughly four-fold since 1776, as steam engines, automobiles, and electric power have revolutionized almost every aspect of daily life. Now the world is moving past the Industrial Revolution into an age dominated by computers, robots, and information networks. This new age will surely produce changes in energy use as fundamental as any that occurred in the past.

The Industrial Revolution, symbolized by this depiction of a New York iron foundry, began a new era in man's use of and dependence on energy sources.

A famous Greek myth centers on Prometheus, above, who stole fire from the heavens and gave it to man.

Before there was home, there was hearth. No one knows when humans first began to use naturally occurring fires. But it must have taken thousands of years before they overcame their deep animal fear of being burned and started tending the mysterious flames. Then, about 700,000 years ago, the still-primitive *Homo erectus* discovered the secret of making fire. Life suddenly became more secure and more enjoyable. Fire made it possible for humans to migrate into colder regions of Europe and Asia. And it helped them to survive the periodic ice ages that swept these areas.

Fire was both used and worshiped. As people began to settle down, a fire at the front of a cave dwelling provided warmth, light, a means to cook, and a barrier against wild animals. Torches provided the ability to travel at night. Hunters began setting wildfires to stampede large game for capture or killing. Yet the awe with which prehistoric peoples viewed this wondrous tool remained—and continued into more modern times.

Among the oldest legends of many cultures are those that tell how fire was brought as a gift from the gods or discovered during some heroic adventure. Perhaps the best known of these is the Greek myth of Prometheus.

Prometheus stole fire from the gods and gave it to man, who otherwise would have been left helpless in the world. Eternal flames—in some places fueled by seepage of oil or natural gas—played a major role in ancient religion.

The Importance of Energy

The coming of agriculture, around 8000 B.C., led to the development of village life. This created new uses for fire and a demand for new fuels. By about 6000 B.C., farmers were tending crops and raising domesticated animals in such widely separated places as the Middle East, Southeast Asia, and central Mexico. These agricultural communities used fire to make pottery, which provided a new way to boil water and cook food. Wood was still the most common fuel, but overuse of forests in the Middle East brought about a search for other fuels. The Babylonians, for example, found that asphalt taken from huge surface deposits made a superior fuel for making pottery.

Agricultural civilization brought many inventions that provided ways to use new forms of energy. Around 3500 B.C., the Mesopotamians invented the wheel and the plow. They ushered in the widespread use of animal power. With oxen tilling their fields by pulling crude wooden plows, farmers could make their land more productive and open vast new areas for growing crops such as barley and wheat. The new harvests were so plentiful that towns quickly grew into cities. Food for these communities was brought to market in carts with wooden wheels.

The agricultural revolution had a dramatic impact on the number of people that could support themselves on the earth's farmland. Between 10,000 and 3000 B.C., world population surged from about three million to more than one hundred million people. Equally dramatic was the increase in towns, villages, and cities. Urban life began to depend more and more on the availability of energy. By about 3000 B.C., builders had learned to make mortar for use in construction by heating limestone in wooden fires. In 2500 B.C., the Babylonians began using petroleum for lamps and for waterproofing. And around 1000 B.C., metal workers in Asia Minor learned how to forge iron in furnaces using charcoal fires.

Yet even in these ancient times, the careless use of energy resources probably began to cause great environmental damage. As people in the Middle East burned larger amounts of wood, they destroyed great forests. The land was not re-seeded, and grazing animals ate many young seedlings. Wind and water then eroded the fertile topsoil, turning much of the region into the deserts we know today. Many forests of ancient China were also cut down about the same time, causing serious environmental damage.

For most of recorded history, energy consumption has largely meant either the use of animals to perform heavy work or the burning of wood to produce heat and light for use in the home. But at the same time, human curiosity and inventiveness led humans to find many other ways to use energy.

Empires rose and fell. But potters, blacksmiths, millers, and carriage makers passed on their trade secrets; from one generation to the next in an ever-increasing hoard of knowledge. Many of these trade secrets involved new ways to use en-

For most of human history, animal power has been a primary source of energy. Below, oxen and men are shown extracting oil from olives around 1570.

ergy. Taken together, this knowledge formed the solid foundation upon which the Industrial Revolution of the nineteenth century was eventually founded.

For thousands of years, the most important source of purely mechanical energy was the waterwheel. The earliest known use of waterwheels was in Greece in 85 B.C., where they were used to grind grain. The Romans used their aqueducts to carry water to waterwheels that powered large flour mills.

Man learned early to harness wind energy. At left, a windmill raises water from a well in 1570 in Europe. Wind also powered the great sailing ships, such as the 18th-century British vessels below.

During the Middle Ages, waterwheels gradually spread throughout Europe and the Arab world. They were used to run a variety of simple manufacturing processes, such as pressing wool into felt, sawing wood, and crushing seeds for oil.

During the sixteenth and seventeenth centuries, there was a craze among the wealthy people of Europe for water-powered devices, such as complex fountains with statues that moved and pipe organs that played automatically. By the late eighteenth century, early textile factories used water power to run their machinery. Around the turn of the nineteenth century, Oliver Evans, an American inventor, went a step further and devised an automated, water-powered grain mill. One of the first factories to operate almost completely by machine, this mill near Philadelphia had numerous water-powered machines that did everything from unload sacks of grain to pack flour in barrels.

Running water was not always available to provide power for water wheels. Wind power was used instead, running windmills that ground grain and pumped water from flooded fields. The origin of the windmill is uncertain, but it was probably invented in China. Windmills were used in Persia by the tenth century and in Europe by the twelfth. The picturesque windmills of Holland made it possible to drain water from the many areas of the country that lay below sea level.

But wind energy made a far more important contribution to the spread of civilization. Wind drove the world's sailing vessels for more than five thousand years. Probably it was the Egyptians who invented the sail around 3200 B.C. Within a few centuries, sailing ships were carrying on a thriving trade around the Mediterranean Sea. By the time of the Romans, ships could carry a thousand tons of cargo or as many as a thousand passengers. Viking sailors conquered the North Atlantic before A.D. 1000. By 1525, the best features of various kinds of sailing vessels had been combined to create the full-rigged ships that made global exploration possible.

The age of sail reached its high point during the mid-1800s. America's majestic clipper ships, carrying as many as thirty-five sails, could reach speeds as high as twenty knots.

Early Use of Fossil Fuels

The full potential of fossil fuels was not recognized until the internal combustion engine was invented at the end of the nineteenth century. But for thousands of years before that, people used fossil fuels in a variety of ways. The Chinese piped natural gas through bamboo poles to heat and light their homes before 1000 B.C. By the fourth century, they also burned it to evaporate sea water to produce salt. The Chinese also began mining coal to replace an already shrinking supply of wood, and by about 200 B.C. they were drilling wells for oil. Petroleum was first refined soon after, when Arabs distilled crude oil to produce a superior fuel for lamps.

Archeologists have found evidence of ancient Indian oil wells in Pennsylvania, Kentucky, and Ohio. In what is now Alberta, Canada, Indian tribes used oil from local tar sand deposits for fuel.

Since the earliest times, man has also used solar and geothermal energy—heat from hot springs in the earth. Sometimes these sources of energy have been used for rather curious purposes. Natural hot springs exist in scattered areas around the world. They are relatively rare, but these geothermal sites are long lasting. Some of them have remained popular since ancient times. Roman baths sometimes used geothermal heat. And for American Indians from several tribes, the Tassajara hot springs, high in California's coastal mountains near Big Sur, served as a sacred healing ground for hundreds of years.

Solar energy is now regarded by some as an alternative to other sources of electrical energy, one that does not affect the environment. Ironically, it was once used as an effective instrument of war. During the third century B.C., Greek soldiers set fire to an invading Roman fleet by holding up flat mirrors to reflect the sun's rays. The scheme is attributed to the great mathematician Archimedes. In a more peaceful vein, the early Greeks also took full advantage of what is now called "passive solar" energy. A shortage of firewood brought about by the overcutting of forests led cities to take advantage of solar heating. Streets were laid out to run east and west, so that windows faced south and got the winter sun.

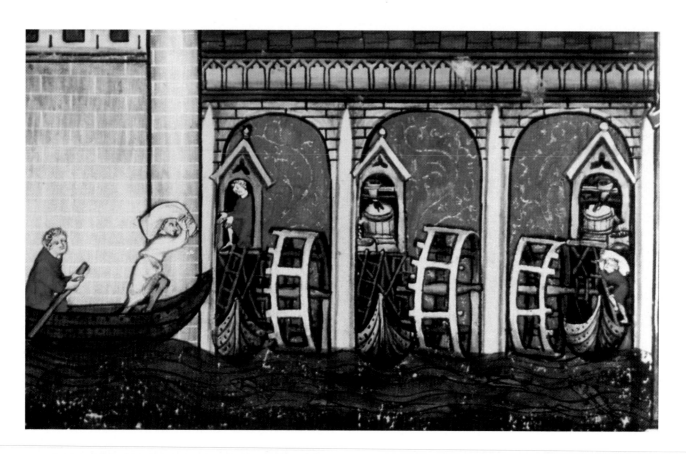

Water was the principal source of energy for industry throughout much of the Middle Ages. In these 13th-century French illustrations, water power is used to grind grain (top) and irrigate fields.

The world has faced periodic fuel shortages—particularly of wood—since ancient times. The shortage of firewood that occurred in sixteenth-century Britain probably had a more lasting effect on human history than any other change from one energy source to another. The shortage led to a shift from the use of wood to coal, which brought about substantial changes in Great Britain's manufacturing and mining industries. These changes, in turn, contributed directly to the birth of the Industrial Revolution.

Coal had been used to some extent as a fuel in Britain during Roman times. Mining of the country's large coal resources began in earnest during the twelfth century. But coal had never been a popular fuel because of its dirtiness. In fourteenth-century London, coal that was burned to heat homes caused dense smog. As a result, King Edward I issued a proclamation forbidding its use under penalty of death. But coal burning continued, particularly as the price of wood began to rise. There were several reasons why the demand for wood began to grow sharply during the early 1500s. First, the art of printing spread throughout Europe. So many documents began to be published that a significant amount of pulpwood was required. Second, advances in metallurgy—that is, making metal from ores—made it easier to produce weapons. This led to the use of large quantities of wood for smelting and refining iron ore. Third, great sailing ships began to explore the world and sail new trade routes. As a result, prime timber for masts and planking became increasingly scarce.

Finally, the population of Great Britain began to grow faster than ever before, nearly doubling between 1530 and 1690. A larger population created new markets in England. It led to the construction of homes and businesses and to the expansion of farms and towns into areas that were previously forested.

By 1600, the shortage of wood became severe. Britain's very lifeline—its great navy and merchant fleets—was threatened by a lack of suitable timber. The government stepped up its efforts to prevent forests from being stripped. Burning coal as a fuel was now looked upon with favor, and coal mining flourished.

At the same time, England developed a number of new technologies in which coal played a major role. This led to even more widespread use of the fuel. Eventually, various advances were introduced that made coal even more useful. One was a process for using coal instead of wood to convert wrought iron into steel. About this time, brickmakers began to bake bricks in coal fires. By the end of the seventeenth century, these advances had lowered the cost of using coal. They also increased production in a number of industrial processes, such as the manufacture of textiles.

Still, what turned out to be the most important advance of all originally had nothing to do with the *use* of coal. Rather, it was an invention designed to provide a better way to drain coal mines. In 1698, a Cornish army officer named Thomas Savery patented a pump that lifted water by condensing steam to create a vacuum, or an absence of air, in a pipe. The water rushed in to fill the vacuum. Savery called his invention simply the "miner's friend." Later generations, however, would mark this rather crude apparatus as the first commercial steam engine *(see Glossary)*.

Actually, Savery's engine didn't work very well. It did not have a piston. All of its valves had to be opened and closed by hand during each cycle. Joints in the metalwork sometimes split because heat melted the solder holding them together. The idea of adding a vertical piston to improve the engine occurred to Thomas Newcomen, a Dartmouth blacksmith.

In Newcomen's engine, steam raised the piston. The piston was connected by a chain and rocker arm to a water pump and through this linkage provided the mechanical energy that worked the pump. Newcomen's engine also had difficulty with melting solder. But sometime around 1705 this caused a lucky accident. On one occasion, water leaked through a gap where the solder had melted. The water suddenly condensed the steam in the cylinder, and this created a vacuum. Air pressure on the other side of the piston pushed so hard that it broke the chain connecting the engine to the pump. The piston then went smashing through the end of the cylinder.

Newcomen recognized this as the breakthrough it literally was. Soon he devised a way to condense the steam with a squirt of water at every stroke. This greatly increased the speed of the piston—and the engine. It also improved the fuel efficiency of the engine.

Newcomen's new engine was an almost instant success. By 1733, there were more than a hundred of them being used to drain mines. But Newcomen's engines were still too slow and wasteful to be used except where large supplies of cheap coal were available.

In 1763, a Scottish instrument maker named James Watt was fixing a model of the Newcomen engine at Glasgow University. Watt was studying the loss of heat that resulted from heating and cooling the entire cylinder during each cycle. His solution, patented in 1769, was to provide a separate unit to condense the steam. This allowed the cylinder and the piston to remain hot. Even in its

Invention of the steam engine marked the start of the Industrial Revolution. Above, a Watt engine pumps water from an English coal mine in the 1790s.

early form, the Watt engine used much less fuel and was far more powerful than Newcomen's engine.

Watt's engine also had a less obvious but equally important asset. The separate condensing unit made it highly versatile. It could be adapted to do many different kinds of jobs. Watt soon discovered how to condense steam on one side of the piston while fresh steam was pushing it on the other side. This double-action principle—and many other ideas Watt incorporated into his designs—transformed the steam engine. It became the first practical means available to industry for converting heat into mechanical energy.

Water-driven machines were then in use for processing textiles. Factory owners quickly converted these water-driven spinning machines to steam power. By 1835, there were 120,000 steam looms in Britain.

Outside Europe, remarkably, industrialization made its greatest strides in the young United States. It was an American inventor, Robert Fulton, who made a major contribution to the Industrial Revolution by building the first commercially successful steamship in 1807.

Six years before Fulton demonstrated his steamship, a Cornish engineer, Richard Trevithick, invented the steam locomotive. For quite a while, industry continued to use stationary engines that pulled freight cars by cable. It was not until 1829 that the first public steam-powered railroad in Great Britain began to run regularly scheduled trains.

In fact, England was in the midst of a revolution created by more efficient use of energy. Its impact had gone far beyond the manufacturing changes brought about by a few men tinkering with machines. Fundamental changes in daily life occurred, and these changes shook the nation's social and economic systems. The increasing use of steam power led to unemployment, and idle workers looking for new jobs crowded into new industrial cities. A growing middle class began to demand the educational and political opportunities that had been reserved for the aristocracy and other privileged groups. During this period of change, some people suffered. But in general, the result was an improved standard of living. It was based on the increased use of energy to produce goods, and it caused the population of Britain to surge—from 6.5 million in 1750 to more than fourteen million in 1830.

What few people realized at the time was that the Industrial Revolution would greatly change the balance of power among nations. A new industrial world was emerging in the West. The nations that led the way in this change needed access to natural resources, such as coal, iron ore, and cotton. They needed a stable form of government. They needed energetic and hardworking citizens. And they needed a desire to take risks and pursue change.

These requirements left many of Europe's leading nations at a disadvantage. Industrial development in France was slowed by the French Revolution and the Napoleonic Wars. Until 1871, Germany was not a united country, but rather a loose collection of small states. Spain was concerned with building a stable government and weakened by the sudden collapse of its overseas empire. One nation, however, enjoyed enough of the needed qualities to take full advantage of the situation. It was the United States that quickly established itself as a leading industrial power.

America and the Industrial Revolution

During the first years of its independence, the United States experienced many of the energy problems that had taken place over centuries in older nations. America's first great energy challenge came during the Revolutionary War. England and Canada cut off vital supplies of coal that America needed to manufacture cannon and other munitions. Fortunately, valuable coal deposits in the United States had been discovered a few years earlier, some of them by a young surveyor

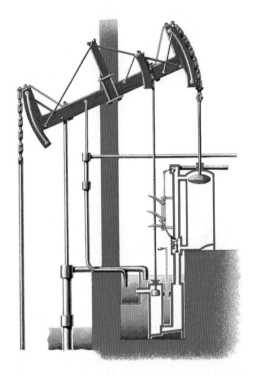

Although he did not invent the steam engine (above), James Watt (below) introduced improvements that made these engines efficient enough for widespread use. He added a separate chamber to condense steam and allow it to push a piston from both sides.

In 1829, England's George Stephenson created a steam locomotive (above) that went so fast—30 miles per hour—it was called the Rocket.

Cotton yarn was manufactured in the textile mill below, one of many mills that operated in New England when the Industrial Revolution reached America.

named George Washington. Domestic mines quickly went into production, and they made a critical contribution to the war effort. For most other purposes, however, coal could not yet compete with easily available wood.

To early settlers, the North American continent appeared to have a wealth of energy in numerous forms. As in England, the textile industry became a leader in the industrial use of energy. America had miles of untouched rivers, and waterwheels became the major source of power during the early part of the nineteenth century. These useful devices drove tens of thousands of looms. Steam engines using coal became more common during this period. But wood was still the major fuel. It was cheap and could be easily transported to mill towns along major waterways. In 1850, wood still represented almost half of U.S. energy consumption. Animal power accounted for more than another third. But the rapid cutting down of forests made it plain that industry would eventually have to rely on fuels other than wood.

Natural gas resources had been recognized since Colonial times. But the first gas well (only twenty-seven-feet deep) was not drilled until 1821. Natural gas was hard to transport over long distances, however, and synthetic gas manufactured from coal remained more popular for illumination during most of the nineteenth century. Until the Civil War, whales also counted as one of America's major energy resources. Whale oil was an important fuel for cooking and lighting. In fact, the United States ranked as the world's leading whaling nation for at least half a century, from the 1830s to the 1880s.

Coal did not become the leading fuel in the United States until the second half of the nineteenth century. It was then that Americans began to use steam-driven railroads to embrace and tame their huge western territories. In 1850, coal accounted for only a small fraction of energy consumption, mainly in the production of coal-gas

---

Whale oil was highly valued as a clean-burning fuel for lamps and cooking. These pictures show whaling in 1745. By the 1830s, America led the world in whaling.

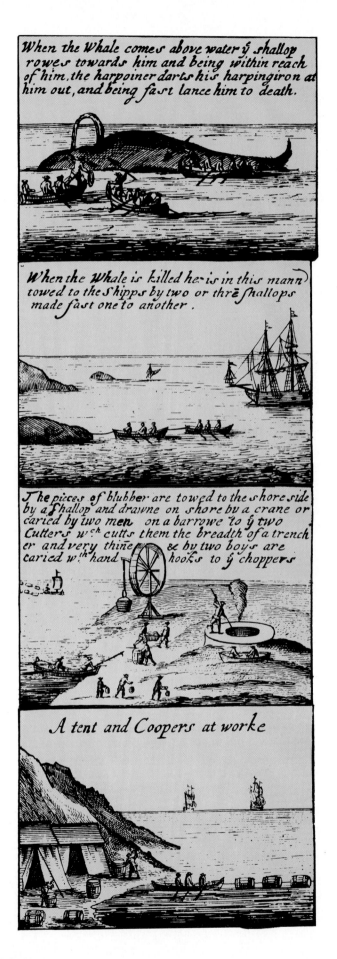

The Bessemer process allowed steel to be made in larger quantities and at lower cost. Above, steel is poured into ingots in a Pennsylvania mill in 1895.

and steel. By 1900 it provided over half the nation's energy. This important change did not result from using coal instead of other fuels in existing industries. Rather, it was the result of finding new uses for coal. More wood was burned as fuel in 1880 than in 1845. But by that time there was a greater need for industrial rather than domestic fuel. Railroads and factories both chose coal as the preferred fuel.

Amazingly, railroads were using twice as much energy as factories. Few would have predicted this result. In 1830, a stagecoach line claimed that horses would be faster and more dependable than locomotives for pulling cars along a track. The stagecoach suggested a race to prove its point, and the horse won. But by 1835 more than a thousand miles of railroad track had been laid in eleven states.

To encourage private investors to extend their railroads into undeveloped areas, the federal government provided a prize. It gave away the one thing it had in abundance—land. Railroad companies received more than 130 million acres of land for laying tracks. The expansion of the railroads across America became a race to see who could lay the most track and get the most land. As a result, the first transcontinental railroad was completed in 1869, less than twenty years after California had been admitted to the Union.

The United States had committed itself to taming a continent. But it was the ingenuity, the inventive skill, of the American people that supplied the technological means to fulfill this ambition. In a burst of creativity, Americans either invented or commercially adapted technologies that revolutionized transportation, agriculture, communication, urban architecture, and daily life. In every case, the effect on energy use was enormous.

America met the first requirement for industrial growth—a good supply of iron and steel. By the 1850s, the United States was competing with Britain in selling iron on the international market. By 1880, American production of pig iron (the raw material cast in blocks) had risen to half that of

Coal mining in the early 1900s was hard, dangerous work (right), but large amounts of this vital fuel were needed by the growing steel mills of Pittsburgh (below) and other industrial cities.

Steel made skyscrapers possible. The earliest skyscrapers were erected in Chicago, beginning in 1883. One of the most unusual is New York City's Flatiron Building, so-called because of its shape. It is seen above during construction in 1901. Tall buildings permitted maximum use of the expensive land in the middle of cities.

Britain. A decade later, the United States was the world's leading producer of pig iron. The introduction of the Bessemer converter and open-hearth furnaces enabled more steel to be produced at lower cost. These new processes provided enough iron and steel to meet even the huge requirements of the rapidly expanding railroads.

Moreover, cheaper steel had found major new uses. By 1880, for example, American farmers were fencing in the great western prairies with more than forty thousand tons of barbed wire each year. This was more than six times the nation's whole production of steel just thirty years earlier. In 1883, the world's first steel-frame skyscraper was built in Chicago, and this city went on to become a center of skyscraper development.

Now there was a need to provide communication over the large distances of the sparsely settled country. As a result, inventors began to consider practical uses for electricity, which had previously remained a curiosity. In 1844, Samuel Morse tapped out his famous message, "What hath God wrought!" to demonstrate his telegraph. Seventeen years later, the first transcontinental telegraph went into operation. Alexander Graham Bell demonstrated the telephone at the 1876 Centennial Exposition in Philadelphia. Eight years later, the first long-distance telephone service between New York City and Boston was begun.

Electric arc lamps were also displayed at the Centennial Exposition. But it was Thomas Edison who revealed the possibilities of electric power by introducing in 1879 the incandescent lamp (today's light bulb). Unlike arc lights, the incandescent lamp was inexpensive, easy to maintain, and could be used in the home. Within three years, the first large coal-fired generators were supplying electricity to an incandescent lighting system for lower Manhattan. By 1895, the mighty Niagara Falls hydroelectric installation had begun operation. The enormous size and complexity of the Niagara project showed that the electrification of America was an achievable goal.

Now America was poised to usher the world into the climax of the Industrial Revolution—the age of oil. Once again, it was a burst of Yankee ingenuity that led the way, putting the world on wheels.

"It Makes a Light"

The invention of the incandescent lamp by Thomas Edison (top, right) in 1879 signaled the beginning of a new energy era. As the sketch, center, from his notebook shows, the device was quite simple, but it took many years to find just the right materials to make a filament that would not be quickly destroyed by the heat as electricity passed through it. Earlier electric lights had used arcs, which required a lot of power and constant maintenance. Edison's lamp was an instant success. The New York Herald proclaimed: "It Makes a Light, Without Gas or Flame, Cheaper Than Oil." Within a few years, large electrical generators were being built throughout the country, and city streets began to glow brightly at night.

During his lifetime, Edison, who was born in Milan, Ohio, in 1847, received 1,093 patents for his inventions and helped establish the tradition of modern industrial research. In 1882, he built the Pearl Street power-generating station in lower Manhattan to supply electricity for New York's First District. Soon electric wires were a common sight along city streets (below is a view of New York's Grand Street), marking the end of the gaslight era. At first Edison used only direct current—that is, electricity that always flows in one direction. Soon, however, George Westinghouse demonstrated the advantages of alternating current for long-distance transmission.

CHAPTER 5

The Age of Oil

By the early years of the twentieth century, the Industrial Revolution had produced profound changes in daily life in America. Towns and cities bustled with new factories. Thousands of miles of railroads tied these towns and cities together, providing a reliable way to travel and to ship goods to almost every corner of the land, including the regions still being settled in the West.

Twentieth-century Americans could take pride in a flood of new inventions, from the telephone and the incandescent lamp to the phonograph and the motion picture camera. These innovations stimulated the popular imagination and led people to expect other equally exciting technological advances.

The automobile was just such an advance—a vehicle that represented a revolutionary new way for the average citizen to get around. The internal combustion engine had already demonstrated its potential as a source of power for this new kind of vehicle *(see Glossary, Internal Combustion Engine).* But there was a problem. The early hand-crafted cars were expensive, and only the wealthy could afford to buy them.

One American car builder, Henry Ford, saw the problem clearly. He was convinced that if he could produce an automobile cheap enough for ordinary citizens to afford he would be able to sell thousands. The answer, he decided, was mass production. He set out to adapt another revolutionary technological advance, the electric motor, to car production. When Ford began to make inexpensive cars on an electrically driven assembly line, he achieved success beyond his dreams. He put America and then the world on wheels, and launched a new chapter in the search for energy—the age of oil.

The Strathcona refinery, located just ten minutes from downtown Edmonton, Alberta, makes 800 petroleum products with minimal environmental impact.

Henry Ford adopted mass-production methods to meet the demand for his cars. Above, Model-A's come off a Lexington, Kentucky, assembly line.

The Rise of the Automobile

To someone living in an increasingly congested city at the turn of the century, the horse and buggy hardly presented a romantic picture, as is sometimes thought today. Horses were not fast enough or powerful enough to meet the growing transportation needs of a modern urban society. They had to be fed and cared for, and their excrement was becoming a serious public health problem. In Chicago at the turn of the century, for example, some 83,330 horses were producing more than 900 tons of manure each day! Something clearly had to be done, and civic groups began to call for banning horses from cities altogether.

Even in smaller towns and on the farm, horses could not keep up with the pace of modern life. People in the rural areas of such a large country needed faster ways to travel. Farmers needed something more powerful than a team of horses to drive the new equipment that could cultivate and harvest their crops more efficiently. And remote communities could not rely entirely on railroads to transport freight to and from distant markets.

The search for a self-propelled road vehicle to replace the horse had already been going on for more than a century, with steam as the favored source of power. The first such vehicle was a three-wheeled steam tractor for hauling cannon, built in 1769 by a French army captain. By the mid-1830s, steam-driven buses were providing regular passenger service in England. Steam also provided the power for the earliest automobiles, beginning in the mid-1860s.

In 1900, most of the 23,000 automobiles registered in the United States were steam-driven, although the battery-powered electric car was gaining popularity. Steam and electric cars were able to command a loyal following even after the internal combustion engine became popular. The Stanley Steamer was manufactured until 1924.

But the contest between steam and electricity on the one hand and gasoline on the other was fundamentally uneven. Steam cars were hard to start and used large amounts of fuel. And they could not generate enough steam for long-distance travel. Electric cars were even more limited. They generally had a top speed of less than twenty miles per hour and a driving range of about fifty miles.

By contrast, the internal combustion engine, running on gasoline, was easy to start and converted heat into mechanical energy more efficiently. In addition, gasoline had a high "heat value." Burning a pound of gasoline yields 21,400 BTUs of energy. Burning a pound of wood produces only 6,900 BTUs. Based on these heat values, a wood-burning car would have to carry more than three times as much fuel to go the same distance as a car that burned gasoline. No wonder gasoline-powered automobiles replaced the earlier steam-driven models!

The first reliable gasoline engine similar to that used in today's cars was developed in Germany in 1876 by Nikolaus Otto. A few years later, it was installed in practical vehicles by his countrymen Gottlieb Daimler and Karl Benz. In 1895, the Duryea brothers, Charles and Frank, established the first American company for making gas-powered cars. That year they drove one of their cars to victory over various European cars in the round-trip Race of the Century between Chicago and Evanston, Illinois, pocketing a $10,000 prize.

Nevertheless, at this point, automobiles were a relatively expensive luxury, available only to a privileged few. A horse and buggy remained the major means of personal transportation for the average American family.

Two changes were needed before gasoline-powered cars would be affordable to most Americans. A new and less expensive way of making automobiles had to be developed, and the price of gasoline had to fall.

The world's greatest "gusher" erupted on January 10, 1901, at Spindletop Field near Beaumont, Texas, signaling the discovery of a vast oil resource.

Enter Henry Ford and his assembly line. Ford's mass production methods made the "family car" a reality, and the effect was startling. Before Ford introduced the Model-T in 1908, even a cheaper car could cost $2,500 or more—as much as some houses. The first Model-T was priced at $850 in 1908. Ford thought this price was too high, although he had sold all of the 6,000 cars he produced. In 1913, when he began turning out his Model-T's on an assembly line, Ford was in a position to achieve his goal—to "democratize the automobile." In 1916, a Model-T cost only $360, and sales that year jumped to 577,036. By 1920, the United States had more than eight million cars on the road, with Fords leading the way.

Henry Ford brought new efficiency to mass production by combining several earlier innovations. The Olds company had used the assembly-line method for producing cars as early as 1902. Parts were carried on platforms that were wheeled from one worker to another. The Cadillac Automobile Company had pioneered the use of interchangeable parts in its cars. Previously, cars contained at least some parts that were custom-built.

Ford improved on all this by setting up his electrically driven assembly line. On Ford's line, vehicle frames on conveyer belts moved past each worker, who installed completely interchangeable parts brought by other conveyer belts. The electrically powered factory was designed around the flow of work. Unlike steam-driven machinery, electrically driven machinery could be arranged so that each step in the manufacturing process was done in order, from first step to last. Ford's new method of production cut the time required to assemble a Model-T from about a day and a half to just over an hour and a half.

But something else was needed now that automobiles had become more affordable—plenty of cheap fuel to power them. In a fortunate coinci-

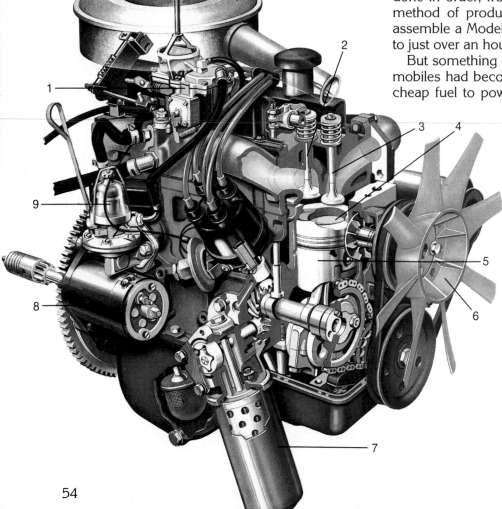

The internal combustion engine enabled automobiles to travel long distances using relatively small amounts of petroleum. A four-cylinder version is seen here. It works by mixing gasoline with air in a carburetor (1) to prepare an explosive vapor that pushes a piston (4). The vaporized fuel passes through a valve (2) into a cylinder (5), where it is ignited by a spark plug. Movement of the piston causes a crankshaft, connected to the car's wheels, to turn. Exhaust gases are ejected through a second valve (3) as each piston returns to its original position after firing. Other key parts are the fan (6), oil filter (7), motor (8), and fuel pump (9).

dence, two things happened at this time to make possible a large supply of cheap gasoline.

One was the discovery in 1901 of the first major Texas oil field. The event was appropriately dramatic—a "gusher" erupted at a drilling derrick in the Spindletop Field near Beaumont. When the size of the discovery became apparent, full-scale production began. More new fields were found in Texas and other western states. As a result, there was a plentiful supply of crude oil to meet the demand created by wider use of the automobile.

The second development that served to make gasoline cheaper was the discovery of a new method of refining crude oil. Before automobiles came into general use, crude oil mainly provided kerosene for lamps. To obtain kerosene, crude oil was distilled and separated into components, or "fractions." These fractions vaporized at different temperatures. The "light" fractions, composed of the smallest molecules, vaporized more easily than the heavier ones.

One of the lightest fractions, gasoline was produced essentially as a by-product of the process that produced kerosene. Gasoline was too volatile to be used in lamps—it might explode. In fact, before it became popular as a motor fuel, it was sometimes dumped into a convenient river.

Only a small proportion of crude oil was turned into gasoline in the refining process. As it happened, the demand for gasoline as an automobile fuel rose just as the demand for kerosene fell sharply because of the growing popularity of the electric light. Now there was a clear need to find a better way to refine crude oil, one that increased the amount of gasoline that could be obtained.

A young chemist named William M. Burton solved this problem in 1913. Aided by his assistant, Robert E. Humphreys, Burton found a way to break up, or "crack," larger molecules of crude oil into smaller, more volatile ones. The process used intense heat and pressure to increase greatly the proportion of gasoline that was produced. Before this discovery, one hundred barrels of crude oil produced only about eleven barrels of gasoline. After the thermal-cracking process became commercially available, the amount of gasoline produced rose to twenty-five barrels in 1918.

"Colonel" Edwin L. Drake (in top hat) stands at the site of the first commercial oil well, which he drilled in 1859 near Titusville, Pennsylvania.

Now the way was open for oil companies to keep pace with the rising demand for cheap gasoline created by the rising popularity of the automobile. Before 1900, ten times more wood than oil was used to supply energy in America. Between 1900 and 1910, demand for oil rose five-fold. Then it more than doubled during each of the next two decades. The number of cars in America also kept rising steadily. And so too did the amount of gasoline each vehicle consumed per week (except for one year during the Great Depression). In other words, people bought more cars and also used them more. Increasing numbers of cars driven an increasing number of miles led to a demand for better roads. These, in turn, helped push truck hauling ahead of rail freight by 1930. The railroads themselves helped to swell the demand for oil by turning to diesel-electric engines, which were cheaper to run than steam locomotives.

Development of the Oil Industry

The rise of the automobile industry created an enormous demand for petroleum as a fuel. But the search for petroleum in the United States actually began in earnest more than half a century before Henry Ford's Model-T's began to roll off the assembly line. Petroleum, in fact, was used in the United States as early as Colonial times. The colonists distilled fuel for their lamps from petroleum that seeped from salt wells or was skimmed

off ponds and streams. In the 1850s, prospectors hoped to find supplies of petroleum that would provide a cheaper alternative to whale oil, which was favored as fuel for lamps because it was almost smokeless.

The first well that was deliberately designed to tap an underground petroleum deposit was drilled in the summer of 1859, near the site of a natural oil seepage on the banks of Oil Creek near Titusville, Pennsylvania. The man in charge of the project was Edwin Laurentine Drake, a retired railroad engineer, who had been hired by a group of investors. His drilling crew consisted of a blacksmith and his two sons.

Drake's plan was simply to punch a hole through the ground by repeatedly raising and dropping an iron bit. The power came from an old steam engine. The crew soon ran into so many problems that the well became known as Drake's Folly. The bit moved speedily enough through the soft ground at first, but the hole kept caving in and flooding.

Drake overcame this difficulty by driving an iron pipe into the ground to serve as a casing. Then the crew found themselves slowly pounding away through solid rock. But they persisted, and at a depth of sixty-nine and a half feet, the drill broke through to a sandy layer that oozed oil. Drake installed a pump, and the well began producing oil at a rate that varied from ten to thirty-five barrels a day.

However modest this well may seem by today's standards, Drake's accomplishment was a major one. He had proved that underground reservoirs of oil could be successfully tapped. Soon thousands of wells dotted the western Pennsylvania hills. In 1861, the same year the first refinery in the region began to operate, the price of oil dropped from $20 a barrel to 10 cents a barrel. Four years later, the first railroad tank car and the first oil pipeline were used to move the "black gold" to market more quickly. The use of kerosene got an extra boost during the Civil War, when many whal-

The New Oil Field **is the title of the illustration at left, made in 1882.**

ing vessels were sunk. From the early 1880s on, petroleum became the fourth largest U.S. export, its importance triumphantly conveyed by the slogan, "oil for the lamps of China."

At first, wells were drilled mainly near locations of surface seepage, as Drake's had been. Then came a generation of prospectors that relied on "doodlebugs"—contraptions ranging from a simple dowsing rod to an elaborate electrical device carried about in a shrouded sedan chair. As their experience grew, however, oil men began to recognize the telltale signs of surface sedimentary rocks that might indicate a petroleum deposit below. Eventually, the oil industry turned to professional geologists, who judged the prospects for further drilling in a more scientific way—for example, by examining core samples obtained from test wells.

As the oil industry developed, it came to be dominated by large corporations, unlike the coal industry, which still has many family-run mines. There were several reasons for this. Drilling was both expensive and uncertain—the sort of high-risk, high-gain investment that required major financial commitment. In addition, many individual steps were required to bring petroleum products to market, from well-drilling to transportation, refining, and distribution. John D. Rockefeller was one of the first businessmen to realize the advantages of combining these functions into a single company. He founded the Standard Oil Company, which had its own refining, pipeline, and marketing facilities.

Finding New Petroleum Resources

Today's large, highly integrated oil companies play an important role in finding, producing, and marketing petroleum products in a reliable and efficient way. Oil exploration has become a highly complex process. Major discoveries are now being made in some of the less developed parts of the world, but huge amounts of capital are required to locate and use these new reserves. Large American oil companies have the financial resources to provide this capital. They also have the technical knowledge and practical experience needed to manage such a large-scale operation.

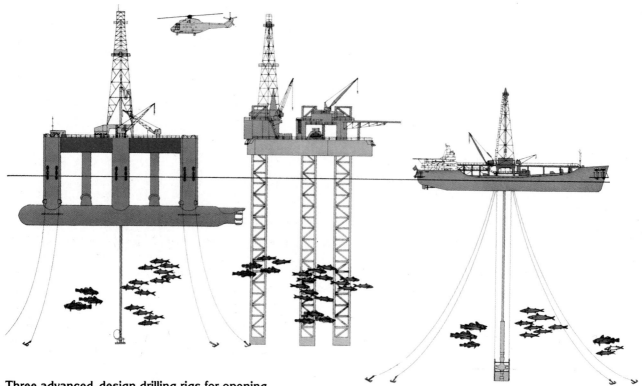

Three advanced-design drilling rigs for opening offshore oil fields: the semisubmersible rig (left), mounted on pontoons, is used for exploratory drilling in rough waters. Self-elevating, or "jack-up," drilling rigs (center) are widely used in water depths of less than 300 feet. A drill ship (right) is moored by anchor lines fastened to a rotating turret so that it can head into prevailing winds and currents while staying in position over the well. Helicopters frequently transport personnel to rigs.

The search for oil is also moving into less accessible areas, where even greater investments must be made in exploration and production. About half of the world's undiscovered oil reserves are believed to lie under the ocean floor. Huge production platforms must be built to tap these deposits. These platforms will rank as some of the largest, most expensive objects ever constructed. Rugged Arctic wastelands have also become frontiers for oil exploration. The largest oil field in North America is at Prudhoe Bay in northern Alaska—closer to the North Pole than to the lower forty-eight states. Developing these difficult new oil resources will demand unprecedented amounts of money. It will also require ingenuity and major technological advances as well.

Petroleum deposits are difficult to locate and to develop because of the way they were formed. Petroleum reserves began millions of years ago as decaying organic material at the bottom of ancient lakes and seabeds. The action of bacteria removed oxygen and nitrogen from this organic matter. This enriched the carbon and hydrogen content of these sediments. As more layers were built up, heat and pressure increased. This supported chemical reactions that further transformed the organic sediments into a variety of different hydrocarbons, molecules rich in hydrogen and carbon. This accounts for the complex mixture of compounds that petroleum contains. These include asphalt, lighter fractions such as kerosene and gasoline, and natural gas, or methane.

Most of the petroleum ever formed was lost due to natural processes, mainly seepage of liquid into the surrounding earth. The oil fields that remain have resulted from relatively rare geological accidents. When hydrocarbons were formed near a layer of porous rock, they would sometimes accumulate near the top of the layer (see Glossary, Hydrocarbons). They were forced upward by the pressure of water underneath. This is not really a "pool" of oil, as some people believe. Rather it is a layer of oil-saturated porous rock covered by a denser layer of rock that prevents the further movement of the hydrocarbon molecules.

The conditions of its formation make oil a limited resource, concentrated in a few widely scattered deposits. To find rock layers with their trapped oil and gas, geologists first look for clues on the land surface that suggest appropriate rock formations below. During early exploration in the western United States, one of the most useful of these clues was the "sheepherder anticline," a ring of cliffs that offered protected grazing for sheep. The cliffs also showed that the earth's surface had been pushed up in a way that could create a trap for oil in the sedimentary layers underneath. The use of photographs from earth satellites has now greatly enhanced the ability of scientists to look for such telltale surface formations in many places around the world.

Once a likely area has been found, scientists conduct surveys that provide a more detailed picture of rock formations beneath the surface. Sound waves created by explosives or by a truck-mounted vibrator bounce off layers of rock as deep as thirty thousand feet and are detected by devices called geophones. Geologists can interpret the pattern of these reflections to pinpoint the thickness and structure of various layers. To map undersea rock formations, sound waves are created by ejecting bursts of compressed air from a "sleeve exploder" towed by a research vessel. Reflected waves are then detected by the vessel's hydrophones and analyzed in much the same way they are on land.

Considerable art and science have thus already been applied to exploration even before the first well is dug at what looks like a promising location. Long experience has taught the men and women involved in the search to place no bets until the drill is sunk. Even with the best preparations, only one "wildcat" well in six finds an undiscovered accumulation of oil and gas. Only one in fifty taps a significant deposit. Sometimes stratigraphic test wells are also drilled to provide geologists with samples of different layers of earth. Particularly important are the tiny fossils present in sedimentary rock brought up from a test well in a core sample. These finds can help establish the age of various layers of rock. After a petroleum reserve has been discovered, three or four "confirmation" wells are generally needed to determine the limits of the deposit.

Producing Oil in Remote Regions

Such advanced methods of locating new petroleum deposits must be used because most of the

Braving the stormy waters of the North Sea, a semisubmersible drilling rig searches for oil off the Shetland Islands of Great Britain.

world's easily produced oil has already been found. Most new discoveries are located in isolated regions of the world. Oil companies must also develop a variety of improved techniques for producing oil from these new deposits.

Some of the new oil is found in the Arctic, where the physical landscape is harsh and difficult. Much of the land in oil-rich regions of the far north is covered to a great depth with "permafrost," a frozen mixture of water, soil, and rock. In summer, when work in the fields reaches a frantic level, the top few feet of the permafrost may melt and cause vehicles to become mired. Sometimes work pads must be constructed on layers of insulation to keep them from sinking. Similarly, when the eight-hundred-mile Trans-Alaska Pipeline was built to connect Prudhoe Bay to Valdez, the nearest ice-free port, special cooling devices had to be installed in some spots to keep the pipeline from melting the permafrost beneath.

Arctic conditions can push both humans and equipment to their limits. In northern Alaska, the sun may not rise above the horizon for more than eight weeks a year. Yet work schedules go on

The search for oil takes petroleum experts to all corners of the world. Above, exploratory wells in the Empty Quarter of oil-rich Saudi Arabia.

The Trans-Alaska Pipeline (below) carries petroleum nearly 800 miles from Prudhoe Bay to the ice-free port of Valdez, on Prince William Sound.

around the clock. Temperatures may fall to minus 68 degrees Fahrenheit—low enough to cause metal to crack. For this reason, truck engines may have to be kept running constantly. Snowstorms can drop visibility to zero and produce windchill factors of minus 115 degrees Fahrenheit. And, of course, virtually no supplies are available locally. Housing for workers on the Trans-Alaska Pipeline had to be shipped from the lower forty-eight states in twelve-ton modules.

The latest Alaskan oil frontier covers the shallow areas of the Beaufort Sea just off the state's northern shore. Here the biggest problem is floating ice, whose movement can crush a conventional drilling platform. Oil companies are trying two solutions to this problem. The first involves hauling gravel to a prospective site to build an artificial island. This is costly, but the resulting gravel island will remain stable for a long time. In very shallow areas, where drilling can be limited to the winter months, an alternative approach has been to thicken the existing ice enough to hold heavy equipment. By repeatedly flooding and freezing an area, oil men build ice structures thirteen hundred feet in diameter and thirty feet thick. (They disintegrate with the spring thaw.)

The other major area for future oil exploration is the deep ocean. Oil companies are now seeking ways to establish production in depths up to two thousand feet, which were previously impractical.

The offshore oil drilling platforms now in place generally operate at depths up to one thousand feet. There are several kinds. Most of the hundreds of offshore platforms that can be seen in the Gulf of Mexico have a basic "steel jacket" type of construction. These platforms are attached to the bottom by piles driven through steel sleeves in the structure and are suitable for relatively calm waters up to one thousand feet deep. In the more severe conditions of the North Sea, "gravity platforms" are favored. They are held down by the enormous weight of a concrete base, which is towed to the site, filled with cement, and sunk.

For depths greater than about one thousand feet, oil companies are using more innovative designs. One is the "guyed tower," a platform that rests on a relatively slender steel tower which is held in place by cables stretching out in all directions. Designed to sway gently, the structure does not require the enormous strength it would need if it were to remain rigid. Guyed-tower platforms may someday be used to reach oil deposits at depths of two thousand feet.

As an alternative to building a whole platform in very deep water, oil companies may use a "submerged production system." This complex structure rests on the ocean floor. It is able to guide drilling shafts lowered from a surface ship. It also can accommodate wellhead assemblies to allow oil to flow from completed wells.

These are just some of the ways in which oil companies are trying to find new petroleum resources. The need is great. Petroleum is expected to remain America's single most important fuel for the rest of this century. When demand reached a peak, during the late 1970s, oil provided just under half of all the energy consumed in the United States. It is expected to account for at least one-third of total energy use in the year 2000. If current forecasts hold true, more than one-third of the oil and gas the world will need in the year 2000 has yet to be discovered.

The age of oil is far from over. In the twentieth century, petroleum provided the energy-rich fuels that brought people new freedom. Petroleum made it possible for twentieth-century man to wander about distant countrysides in sputtering automobiles and then to span the globe in jet airplanes which transformed nations into neighborhoods. The search for petroleum stimulated great explorations and feats of technological daring.

Petroleum will remain a vital fuel in supplying America's energy needs. Finding the remaining supply that is concealed under the earth's surface and bringing it into production will require great effort. Oil has always been a limited resource. Even today, the exact extent of the remaining supply is not known. The task of discovering and developing this supply will become more difficult and more expensive with each passing year. Because of this, other fuels from the earth—including coal, oil from shale, and gas from deep deposits—will play an increasingly significant role in maintaining America's energy supply.

CHAPTER 6

The Energy Future: Fuels from the Earth

Petroleum has unique advantages as a source of energy. It is convenient. Large amounts of oil can be stored or transported by truck, train, ship, or pipeline. It is versatile. Crude oil can be refined into many different products that perform different functions, from fueling vehicles to generating electric power. And it has a high heat value. A relatively small volume of gasoline will power a car or airplane over long distances. All of these advantages make it likely that petroleum will remain the single most important fuel for decades to come.

Until recently, oil has been readily available and relatively cheap to produce. At the time of its peak use in the late 1970s, oil accounted for almost one half of all the energy consumed in the U.S. By 1983, that figure had declined to about 43 percent, mainly because of the significant rise in the price of oil.

That rise occurred largely as the result of one condition: petroleum resources are not evenly distributed around the world. As a result, in 1982 just two countries, Saudi Arabia and Kuwait, accounted for 35 percent of all the world's "proven reserves" of petroleum—that is, crude oil deposits that can be produced commercially. In the same year, the Soviet Union and Iran held 18 percent of the remaining proven reserves. Mexico had 8 percent. The U.S. had 4 percent.

Such a concentration of oil resources, combined with the world's great dependence on petroleum products, represented a high potential for conflict over who should have access to oil and at what price. The conflict became a reality when the oil crisis occurred.

Tar sands, scooped up by this giant machine at the Athabasca site in northeast Alberta, Canada, represent a promising new source of fuel.

The crisis developed in the autumn of 1973 when war broke out between Egypt and Israel. Saudi Arabia halted oil shipments to the United States and several other Western nations. This stoppage decreased the world's oil supply by only 10 percent. But consuming nations immediately experienced shortages, especially of gasoline.

More important in the long run than the shortages, however, was a steady upward spiral of petroleum prices. The Saudi Arabian embargo lasted only six months and then shortages gradually disappeared. But petroleum prices continued to increase at roughly the same rate as inflation. In late 1978, the revolution in Iran led to a new round of shortages. Oil prices rose again, more than doubling. By 1982, the price of imported crude oil had climbed to $34 a barrel. (It was $2.48 a barrel in

1972.) This huge price increase had serious worldwide consequences. Economic growth was slowed in both industrial nations and less developed countries.

The price rise will also have an effect on the development of energy resources in future years. For one thing, it has made plain the need for conservation in order to accomplish two goals: first, the reduction of the total amount of energy consumed and second, the more efficient use of that energy. Conservation will save money as well as resources, and it can go a long way toward making future energy shortages less likely to occur.

Many countries have already made great progress in energy conservation. After world oil consumption peaked in 1979, it fell 14 percent during the following four years. Improved fuel efficiency

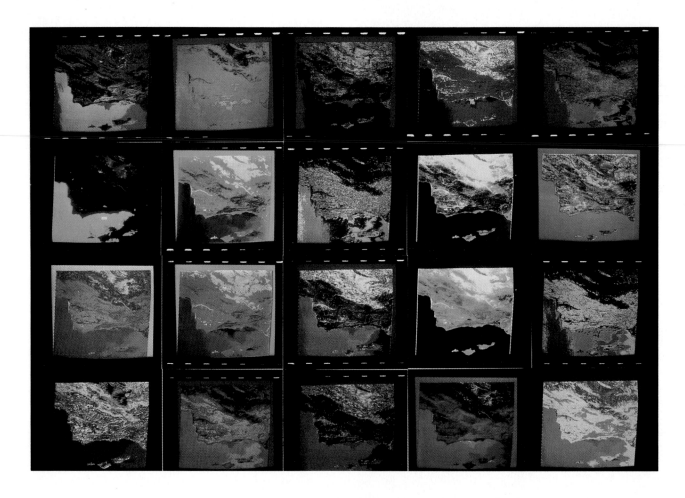

in automobiles played an important part in this drop. Improved insulation and better management of heating systems in homes and businesses also contributed to energy conservation. As a result of this and other conservation measures, the amount of oil used each day for heating in the United States declined 43 percent from 1973 to 1983.

At the same time that conservation has taken hold, there has been a shift away from the use of petroleum. Oil consumption by electric utilities peaked in 1978, then dropped significantly; in 1983 it was just 39 percent of its peak 1978 level. Nearly all this reduction came from increased use of coal to generate electricity.

Solving the Energy Challenge

As promising as these trends are, they will not solve the energy challenge America faces in the years ahead. For America to experience steady economic growth, it will need to augment its vital petroleum resources with additional supplies of energy from other sources.

To understand the contribution that these other energy resources are capable of making to our energy needs, we should remember that there are three basic areas of energy consumption: (1) fuels for transportation; (2) fuels for heating homes and commercial and industrial establishments; and (3) energy to power industrial processes.

As we move toward the year 2000 and on into the twenty-first century, limited supplies of petroleum will be used more and more to provide energy that no other source can provide as conveniently and efficiently. Primarily, this comes down to fuel for transportation. As we have seen, the use of oil for generating electricity has declined sharply. This trend will continue, although at a reduced pace.

While petroleum will remain an important source of energy, fossil fuels other than petroleum will also make a significant contribution to Ameri-

The thermograph above, taken with infrared light, shows where heat leaks from a home. White, yellow, and red indicate the greatest heat losses. Such leaks can waste up to a third of a home's fuel.

ca's energy needs. And two other categories of energy resources will supply vital energy needs in the years ahead: nuclear power and renewable resources, such as solar and hydroelectric power.

Among the fossil fuels, coal will play a leading role. It supplied about 22 percent of United States energy needs in 1983. The use of coal was heavily concentrated in the generation of electricity. Where liquid or gaseous fuels are required, synthetic fuels produced from coal, oil shale, and tar sands will replace various petroleum products *(see Glossary, Synthetic Fuels)*. But further technological progress is needed to solve environmental and cost problems in the production of synthetic fuels. They will not make a large contribution to the total energy supply until after the turn of the century. Finally, natural gas, which supplied about 25 percent of America's energy needs in 1983, will maintain its place as a leading source of energy.

Computer images of terrain, based on data transmitted by satellites, are the latest tool petroleum engineers use to help find deposits of oil and gas.

In this chapter we will assess the potential contribution of fossil fuels other than petroleum, beginning with natural gas *(see Glossary)*. In succeeding chapters, we will examine nuclear power and renewable resources.

The Role of Natural Gas

Natural gas was formed by the same forces that created petroleum, and it is often obtained along with petroleum from the same deposits. More than half of the demand for natural gas in the United States comes from industry. Natural gas is used as a fuel in processes ranging from glassmaking and the generation of electric power to the removal of fuzz from corduroy. Most of the rest of the gas is used in homes and commercial buildings to provide a particularly clean source of heat.

Natural gas began to make a substantial contribution to the world's energy supply only after World War II, when economical ways to transport it over long distances came into use. Before that time, most of the gas used for cooking, heating, and industrial purposes was manufactured from coal. From the mid-1940s to the mid-1960s, consumption of natural gas in the U.S. nearly quadrupled, to about 30 percent of all energy consumed.

During this period of rapid growth, the price of natural gas sold across state lines was regulated by the Federal Power Commission (FPC). At the price set by the FPC, natural gas was a good buy relative to other sources of energy. In 1953, for example, it was five times more expensive to heat a house with oil than with natural gas. Demand for gas remained high as a result. But producers maintained that their profits were too small to make it worthwhile for them to find new gas deposits. In fact, since 1968, except for one year, more natural gas from existing wells has been sold than has been added to reserves.

As natural gas reserves continued to be reduced, the value of the gas increased. It was not until 1978, however, that legislation was enacted changing the price structure for gas. As a result of this change, exploration for gas increased. Experts

disagree on how many years of natural gas reserves are left to meet future needs. It is estimated that "proven" reserves used at today's level of consumption will last about ten years. Beyond "proven" reserves, there is great uncertainty about the volume of potential reserves. One thing that experts generally agree on is that these reserves will be increasingly difficult to find and develop. Consequently, this gas will be more costly.

America's domestic natural gas resources are surely too limited for gas to replace oil in most uses. But natural gas is far more plentiful in the rest of the world. International natural gas reserves are still being discovered at a higher rate than gas is being extracted from them. The Soviet Union, in particular, has vast untapped deposits of natural gas. These deposits represent about 40 percent of the world's proven reserves. To carry this gas from Siberia to Europe, the U.S.S.R. is now building six fifty-six-inch-diameter pipelines which have a combined length of 12,400 miles. Russian natural gas is already replacing large amounts of oil as an industrial fuel throughout Eastern Europe. Exports to Western Europe may make such substitution possible there by the late 1980s.

Coal: The Primary Transition Fuel

As the world conserves its remaining resources of oil, coal will serve as the primary transition fuel, providing additional needed energy. Coal is expected to account for at least one-third of the energy growth in the world during the next twenty years, and possibly one-half. Its main use will be in generating electricity.

Coal's primary advantage is its abundance. The world's economically recoverable coal deposits contain five times more energy than do proven oil reserves. This is enough coal to sustain present rates of demand for at least two centuries. The United States alone possesses about 250 billion tons of coal that can be mined economically with today's technology. America's coal supply is equal

---

Liquefied natural gas (LNG) is transported under high pressure in five spherical tanks set into the deck of this specially designed ship.

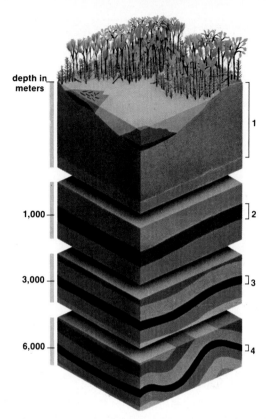

THE FORMATION OF COAL: Decomposed plant material (peat) collects at the bottom of a swamp (1). Increasing pressure turns it to lignite (2), then to bituminous coal (3), and then to anthracite (4).

---

to more than twice the energy in proven Middle Eastern oil reserves. According to a report issued by the World Coal Study, a 1980 meeting of representatives of the leading coal producers, demand for coal is expected to double or triple before the year 2000.

Coal was burned by American Indian tribes long before the arrival of white settlers. The Pueblo Indians, for example, burned coal as a fuel in making pottery. The first commercial coal-mining operations began in 1750, near what is now Richmond, Virginia. With the development of steam-driven electric generators in the 1890s, coal became the undisputed "king of fuels" in America.

By 1900, coal accounted for more than 70 percent of U.S. energy consumption. But after World War II, oil and gas rapidly replaced coal. By 1960, coal had slipped into third place, representing only about 23 percent of America's energy supply. By the early 1970s, coal accounted for only about 17 percent of America's energy supplies. Then, as oil became more expensive after the mid-1970s, the use of coal began to rise again.

Coal occurs in layers, or "seams," in the earth's crust that vary from one inch to one hundred feet or more in thickness. In the United States, the hardest coal, called anthracite, is mainly found in eastern Pennsylvania. It is used chiefly for heating.

Bituminous coal is the most abundant grade. It serves as the main fuel for the generation of electric power; it is also transformed into coke, which is used in steelmaking. (Coke is made from coal that is heated in an oven in the absence of air.) The richest American deposits of bituminous coal lie west of the Appalachian Mountains, in the Ohio River valley. Some bituminous coal is also found in the Great Plains states.

Two other varieties of coal, sub-bituminous and lignite, have a much lower heat content than either anthracite or bituminous coal. Found in the Great Plains states and along the Gulf Coast, they are used mainly as fuels for steam boilers used in generating electricity.

Coals from the eastern United States now represent about 65 percent of total production. In the future, production of western coal is expected to increase. One reason is that western coal generally has a low sulfur content, which means that it produces less pollution when burned. In addition, western coal lies close to the surface and often can be mined by digging huge open pits, a method called surface, or "strip," mining. Surface mining can be less expensive than underground mining, which often involves sinking one or more shafts hundreds of feet into the earth.

As coal burns, the sulfur impurities it contains combine with oxygen to form sulfur dioxide, which constitutes a form of air pollution. This gas can also be produced by automobiles if they burn gasoline or diesel oil containing sulfur. But 98 percent of sulfur dioxide emissions come from nonautomotive burning of fossil fuels. Scientists are working on new technologies for reducing or eliminating the pollution coal can produce, and we will examine these technologies later in this chapter.

Synthetic Fuels from Coal

When coal is first converted into liquid or gaseous synthetic fuels, sulfur dioxide pollution is not a problem because the sulfur is removed during the conversion process, eliminating this form of pollution.

Making synthetic fuels from coal is hardly a modern development. The first synthetic fuel was produced in 1609, when the Belgian chemist and physician Jan van Helmont discovered that heating coal caused a gas to escape.

By 1807, gas manufactured from coal illuminated a city street—London's Pall Mall—for the first time. Soon the gaslight era was in full swing. Cities had their own gashouses to produce fuel for heating and lighting. These facilities closed down as natural gas became more widely available after World War II.

The coal gas used for lighting and heat was manufactured by heating coal. This produced a limited quantity of flammable methane gas, which is also the main component in natural gas. More gases can be produced if coal is exposed to steam and oxygen under high pressure while it is heated, a method called gasification. An advantage of gasification is that the sulfur in the coal reacts with hydrogen in the steam to form a gas. This gas is easily removed so that the remaining gas burns with little pollution.

One version of this gasification method, developed in Germany during the 1930s, is called the Lurgi process. The Lurgi process produces a product called intermediate BTU gas (IBG), which consists of methane, carbon monoxide, and hydrogen. Although intermediate BTU gas has only about 40 percent of the energy content of natural gas, it can be used as an industrial fuel and can also serve as the raw material for making liquid fuels and chemicals.

One drawback in the original Lurgi process is that the gas yield is not very high. In addition, bituminous coals can form a sticky ash that cakes up in the reaction chamber and that could impede the operation.

Now the British Gas Corportion has figured out a way to run the reactor at a temperature high enough to produce a molten slag waste, which is easily removed. Commercial plants using the improved Lurgi process may be built before the turn of the century.

To obtain a higher quality gas than IBG, a catalyst can be added to the process. (A catalyst is a substance that helps promote a chemical reaction but is not itself used up in the reaction.) The cata-

Working Underground

Coal mining has always been difficult, dirty work. Often it was also dangerous, with many miners killed by cave-ins and gas explosions. Conditions have improved substantially, however, since the 1890s when the picture at right was taken. At that time, miners in the United States worked sixty-hour weeks and received little government protection.

Today, underground miners are skilled operators of large, complex machines that can extract from a seam as much as twelve tons of coal every minute—and then automatically load it into shuttle cars. Safety is a primary concern. Electrical devices test the air in mines and warn when gas buildups that might cause explosions are occurring. Steel and concrete are used to strengthen tunnels and prevent cave-ins. But black lung disease, which affects the breathing of miners who have inhaled coal dust for many years, is still a problem. Recent laws limit the amount of coal dust permitted in mine air.

Increasingly, coal in the western part of the United States is expected to come from surface mining, which is less costly than underground mining. Considerable care is being taken to reclaim the land and to prevent environmental damage.

lyst makes more of the carbon in the coal combine with hydrogen to form substitute natural gas (SNG).

In 1971, scientists at Exxon Corporation invented a process to produce substitute natural gas using technology adapted from petroleum refining. A catalyst is added to powdered coal as it is fed into a reaction chamber. In the chamber, all the particles are kept suspended by a jet of steam and hydrogen entering from the bottom. This produces more thorough mixing and reaction as the carbon and hydrogen combine to form a gas.

The process is being tested at an Exxon plant in Baytown, Texas, that processes one ton of coal a day.

Coal can also be used to produce synthetic oil. A Canadian doctor and geologist, Abraham Gesner, patented a process for doing this in 1854. The process involves heating coal and condensing the vapor.

Gesner's oil was suitable for use in lamps and he named it kerosene. But many people called it simply "coal oil."

Later, as the petroleum industry grew during the last half of the nineteenth century, kerosene could be produced more cheaply from crude oil. Since then, only a few countries have used coal as a source of liquid fuel, usually when petroleum was unavailable. During World War II, for example, the Allies cut off German oil supplies, and the German air force had to depend on aviation gasoline that was produced from coal.

With the rising price of crude oil during the 1970s, the economic feasibility of synthetic oil has improved. Making gasoline and other liquid fuels from coal could allow the United States and other countries with large coal resources to sharply reduce their petroleum imports. But achieving this goal would require an enormous expansion of production facilities. At the time of their peak production, the wartime German plants each processed only about six hundred tons of coal per day. Commercial plants now proposed for the United States would have to process twenty-five thousand or more tons of coal a day in order to produce an economically practical amount of synthetic oil.

There are generally two methods of producing oil from coal. One is called the indirect liquefaction process. The first step in this process is to gasify coal to an intermediate BTU gas. Next, a catalyst is added to change the low quality gases into liquids and substitute natural gas.

The indirect liquefaction process yields a variety of products and is most suitable for making chemicals and gas. South Africa has used this process more actively than any other country. By 1984, South Africa expects to fill half its petroleum needs with synthetic oil.

The second method for producing liquid fuels from coal is called the direct liquefaction process. It produces oil by mixing powdered coal with a liquid containing hydrogen. A catalyst is added to sustain the chemical reaction.

A number of American companies are concentrating on perfecting the direct liquefaction process. It has been tested successfully in two pilot plants. One plant, near Catlettsburg, Kentucky, was built by the Ashland Oil Company and several industrial partners. It could convert six hundred tons of coal per day into 1,800 barrels of synthetic oil. It used a specific type of direct liquefaction called the "H-coal" process, which was developed by Hydrocarbon Research, Inc. Another industry

Tar sand, seen at left, is mixed with steam and hot water to release bitumen, a sticky substance that is then distilled to produce synthetic crude oil.

At Syncrude Canada Ltd.'s operation at Athabasca, Alberta (above), newly mined oil sands are dropped onto conveyers that lead to the extraction plant.

group, led by Exxon Corporation, has worked on the development of a direct liquefaction process called the Exxon Donor Solvent (EDS) process. Exxon successfully tested this process at a pilot plant at Baytown, Texas, which had the capacity to convert 250 tons of coal per day into synthetic crude oil.

The H-coal and EDS processes differ mainly in the way that the hydrogen and the catalyst are mixed with the coal. Both of these processes are expected to be ready for use in large commercial facilities before the turn of the century.

No one can estimate what the contribution of synthetic liquid fuels made from coal will be to the total supply of energy in future years. For the near future, attempts to advance and refine the technology involved will continue. The efficiency and economy of this technology will have to be com-

pared to similar technological progress in the production of synthetic liquid fuels from other sources, such as tar sands and oil shale (see Glossary). These natural deposits contain compounds of hydrogen and carbon that can be processed to produce synthetic fuels.

Refining Tar Sands and Oil Shale

Tar sand deposits are sands that contain a thick hydrocarbon called bitumen. Black and sticky, bitumen oozes from the sand on a hot summer's day and hardens like stone in the winter.

Oil shale deposits consist of porous sedimentary rock that contains a hydrocarbon called kerogen. The kerogen is tightly bound in the rock. Even thicker than bitumen, kerogen has the consistency of rubber.

Bitumen and kerogen both can be extracted from the tar sands or oil shale. The liquids that are released can then be refined into synthetic fuels which could be used in transportation and to power industrial processes of various kinds.

In North America, there are large deposits of tar sands in Alberta, Canada, and in Utah, Wyoming, and California. Around the world, the Soviet Union and at least five South American countries have substantial tar sand deposits.

Taken together, these deposits hold the largest accumulation of liquid hydrocarbon in the earth's crust—more than three times the amount of available crude oil in all the world's known petroleum reserves.

Like tar sands, oil shale has long been recognized as a potentially huge source of synthetic fuel. The area around the mutual boundaries of Utah, Wyoming, and Colorado contains about 1,800 billion barrels of shale oil—more than all the petroleum reserves of the Middle East.

Obtaining large amounts of oil from shale in an economic way has frustrated engineers for years. Producing synthetic fuels from oil shale and tar sands involves two major operations: handling huge amounts of raw materials, and disposing of the wastes left over from processing. In spite of these difficulties, a few large projects to develop tar sands are now underway.

Tar Sands. The use of bitumen as a source of energy began before the coming of white settlers to North America; Indians living in Alberta, Canada, burned it as a campfire fuel. The first major development of the deposits to produce synthetic fuel began in 1968 when Great Canadian Oil Sands, Ltd. completed a refining plant that began to produce fifty thousand barrels a day of synthetic crude oil. When the price of petroleum rose during the 1970s, the Canadian government joined with several oil companies to form Syncrude Canada, Ltd., to develop further the tar sand resource. This consortium built a $2.2 billion plant, which opened in 1978. The plant's capacity is about 125,000 barrels of synthetic crude oil a day at the Athabasca deposit in northeast Alberta.

At the Syncrude plant, dredging machines called draglines scoop up eighty cubic yards of tar sands at a time. The sand is then mixed with

To produce oil from shale—the rock that burns (above)—the waxy kerogen in the shale must be crushed and heated. About 47,000 barrels of oil are expected to come daily from the Colorado site at left.

steam and hot water to produce "slurry," a black liquid mixture. In this hot slurry, particles of sand slowly sink to the bottom. The lighter bitumen floats upward through the water to form a frothy layer on top. The bitumen is then heated to 1,000 degrees Fahrenheit and distilled.

The process includes a step in which sulfur is removed. The final product consists of crude oil, solid coke, and a low-quality gas that is used as a fuel at the plant.

Oil Shale. Indian tribes of the western United States called oil shale "the rock that burns," and some pioneers used it to provide grease for their wagon wheels.

For a brief period in the middle of the nineteenth century, a fledgling industry arose to produce kerosene from oil shale. But it could not compete once cheap petroleum became available from oil wells.

After World War II demonstrated the critical importance of oil to national security, the U.S. Bureau of Mines established a facility at Anvil Points, Colorado, to develop the technology needed to produce large amounts of shale oil. In 1957, the Union Oil Company constructed a test plant that was capable of processing one thousand tons of shale per day.

But low petroleum prices forced the plant to shut down its operations the next year. It was not until the late 1970s that the cost of crude oil rose to a high enough level to rekindle an interest in shale oil.

In the process developed by the Bureau of Mines, crushed shale is fed into the top of a chimneylike vessel. The shale is heated by a column of hot gas blowing downward. As the pieces of shale fall to the bottom of the vessel, the kerogen they contain is broken down into oil and gas.

At the bottom, the vaporized oil is condensed and collected. The gas is returned to the top of the vessel, where it is ignited and used to heat the shale.

In this process, large quantities of water are needed for cooling the oil vapor and for disposing of waste. Each barrel of oil recovered requires three barrels of water.

This is a potential problem in the arid regions west of the Rocky Mountains. In addition, as the kerogen is released from the shale, the shale expands to one and a half times its original size. That means the waste is too large to fit into the hole from which the shale was taken.

Environmental concerns such as these have prompted the development of a processing method called "in situ" (Latin for "in place"). In this method, the shale is heated and the synthetic fuel is produced in underground mines dug out of shale deposits. The shale is set on fire in the mine, and the oil is pumped to the surface. The most ambitious project using this complicated process is now being developed by Occidental Petroleum in the rich Piceance Basin oil shale deposit in western Colorado. If the Colorado facility fulfills expectations, the in situ process should use less water and produce less visible waste than a surface oil shale plant.

Clean Energy from Coal

Tar sands and oil shale may someday make a significant contribution to our energy supply. Coal is already doing just that. At the same time, scientists are making intensive efforts to insure that the energy coal supplies is clean energy.

We will now examine the technologies that are being used and are under development to reduce the pollution caused by burning coal. Impurities that burning coal produces can be removed to varying degrees before the coal is burned, during its burning, or after it is burned.

Many power plants today burn coal as it comes from the mine and then remove small particles and noxious gases from the smoke created by the coal fire. But the equipment needed to do this is quite expensive, particularly when it must be installed in an older plant.

Coal can also be cleaned before it is burned, essentially by washing it. This method does not remove the organic sulfur which is uniformly distributed throughout the coal. But cleaning does remove some of the inorganic sulfur which occurs as particles in a variety of shapes and sizes. And it reduces the amount of nonflammable solid material that eventually winds up as ash when the coal is burned.

Coal can also be cleaned as it burns, using a method called fluidized bed combustion *(see Glossary)*. In this process, the sulfur is removed in a chemical reaction. Crushed coal and limestone are fed simultaneously into a power plant's "boiler." This is the vessel where fuel burns and water is boiled to form steam for generating electricity. As the coal burns, calcium from the limestone reacts with the sulfur to form calcium sulfate. This solid substance is then disposed of.

The temperature of the flame in a fluidized bed boiler is lower than that in an ordinary power plant boiler. For this reason, pollution from nitrogen compounds is also reduced. Its advocates claim that fluidized bed combustion will eventually cost less than burning coal and then scrubbing the flue gases. They also maintain that lower grades of coal can be burned using this process without increasing pollution.

The Tennessee Valley Authority has built a prototype fluidized bed power plant near Paducah, Kentucky, which began operation in May 1982. It generates twenty megawatts of electricity, compared to a large commercial coal or nuclear power plant, which generates more than one thousand megawatts.

As this comparison indicates, fluidized bed equipment will have to be enlarged before this technology can produce major amounts of elec-

tricity. Engineers believe that a two-hundred-megawatt fluidized bed plant could be constructed in the late 1980s if the prototype performs well. Eventually, such plants could burn municipal and agricultural wastes as well as coal.

In producing electricity from coal, pollution can also be reduced by using a clean-burning synthetic gas made from the coal. Gasifying the coal and then shipping it to the power plant would be costly, however, and a large amount of potentially usable energy would be lost.

This drawback is overcome in an integrated gasification combined cycle (IGCC) plant *(see Glossary)*. In this process, the heat produced in making the synthetic gas is used to produce steam for generating electricity. The synthetic gas created in an integrated gasification combined cycle plant has a temperature of 2,300 degrees Fahrenheit. It must be cooled to about 100 degrees Fahrenheit in order to remove its sulfur impurities. If a steam turbine is situated next to the gasifier, the heat given off by the cooling gas can be used to create steam that generates electricity.

After the cooled gas has had its sulfur removed, it can also be used to produce electricity in a gas turbine. When it leaves this turbine, the gas is again quite hot, about 1,000 degrees Fahrenheit. The heat from this gas can then be used to produce steam.

The combination of steam and gas turbines enables the plant to generate electricity with a minimum loss of energy. An integrated gasification combined cycle plant is also expected to need only about 65 percent of the water required to operate a conventional coal-fired power plant. This makes it particularly suitable for use near coal mines in arid regions of the United States.

Fluidized bed combustion (right) provides an efficient way to burn coal cleanly. Sulfur compounds, which can cause pollution, are removed from the coal as it burns—they combine with calcium from limestone that is fed into the burner. The particles of coal and limestone are kept suspended by air blown into the burner from the bottom. The waste product, calcium sulfate, is removed as a solid for disposal.

A one-hundred-megawatt integrated gasification combined cycle plant began operation during 1984 at the Cool Water power station of the Southern California Edison Company, near Barstow, California. The plant consumes one thousand tons of coal a day, brought by rail from a Utah mine five hundred miles away. Utility engineers consider the Cool Water plant to be a forerunner of large commercial facilities that could be built in the late 1980s.

A final advantage of the integrated gasification combined cycle technology is that it is very effective in reducing pollution. An IGCC plant meets pollution regulations even more stringent than those now in effect. The California Edison Cool Water facility removes 97 percent of the sulfur from synthetic gas before it is burned. Later plants could remove 99 percent.

There is another way to generate electricity from coal using synthetic fuel. It is based on the fuel cell technology that was originally developed for the space program. Here, too, the trick in keeping the cost down is to avoid wasting heat. The process is relatively simple. Inside a fuel cell, a catalyst breaks hydrogen atoms away from a gaseous fuel. The hydrogen atoms combine with oxygen in a chemical reaction. Combustion does not occur. The movement of free electrons created by the chemical reaction causes electricity to flow from two metal electrodes at either end of the cell. The process is very clean and uses fuel very efficiently. The major waste products are all harmless—water, nitrogen, and carbon dioxide.

Fuel cells are still too small and too expensive for widespread use in power plants. The largest one now operating is a 4.5-megawatt unit located in downtown New York City. Completed in 1982, this fuel cell facility supplies power to the Consolidated Edison Company system. The fuel for this plant is naptha, which is produced from petroleum. But fuel cells are potentially capable of using a wide variety of fuels. Fuel cell power plants using fuels made from coal could be built by the late 1980s. Such plants could provide a more acceptable way of generating electricity in congested urban areas, where safety and freedom from pollution are important considerations.

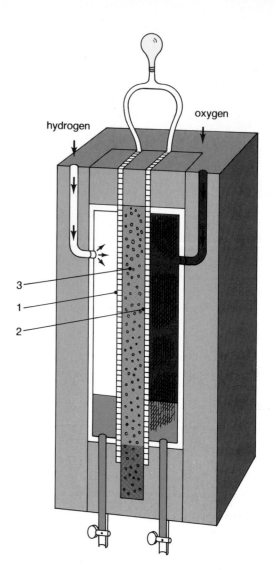

A fuel cell contains two gas chambers, a platinum-coated wire anode (1) and cathode (2), and a thin electrolyte-saturated membrane (3). Hydrogen and oxygen are used to create a chemical reaction that produces electricity with no burning. Heat and hot water are by-products of the reaction.

Long-Term Pollution Problems

The problem of pollution has led to concern about two longer-term effects associated, in part, with burning fossil fuels. One is commonly called "acid rain," although acid deposition is a more accurate term since it can be either "wet" (rain, snow, etc.) or "dry" (particles). Some scientists believe sulfur and nitrogen pollutants released by the burning fossil fuels, including coal, are among the major causes of acid rain (see Glossary, Acid Rain).

The problem of acid rain might, in part at least, be solved by increased use of advanced coal technologies. The buildup of carbon dioxide could not be solved by these technologies, since it is not now possible to burn fossil fuel without producing carbon dioxide.

The term "acid rain" is misleading in another sense because even normal rain is acidic. When carbon dioxide in the air dissolves in the moisture of clouds, it forms a weak acid called carbonic acid that showers the earth in the drops of water that fall as rain. Problems occur when other substances in the atmosphere—sulfur dioxide, nitrogen oxides, and hydrogen sulfide—are also dissolved to form sulfuric or nitric acids in rain. Sometimes these substances come from natural sources, such as volcanoes. But since the Industrial Revolution, more of these substances have been released into the atmosphere as pollution caused by the burning of fossil fuels.

A study conducted from 1973 to 1975 by the Organization for Economic Cooperation and Development (OECD) showed that acid rain might be getting more severe in most of northwestern Europe. The record is less clear in the United States. Measurements are being made all over the northeastern U.S., but the scientific data is not yet complete. In 1980, Congress established a task force, including the Environmental Protection Agency and a number of other governmental agencies, to study the problem of acid rain and, if necessary, to develop ways to reduce or eliminate it. The task force will continue its work for ten years and will issue annual reports to Congress.

A number of private organizations are also conducting major studies of acid rain. One reason for launching so many studies is the need to explain the complicated relationship, if any, between pollution entering the atmosphere from, say, a power plant in Ohio and the death of fish in a lake which may be receiving acid rain in upper New York state. Pollutants can undergo chemical changes as they pass through the atmosphere. After rain has fallen, the ability of soils in different regions to neutralize the acid varies greatly. The point is that scientists do not fully understand the mechanism that produces acid rain. New technologies to control pollution may help to minimize the problem of acid rain. But until scientists understand more about how acid precipitation is formed, it is not clear how much effect new pollution standards would have in preventing environmental damage.

The other long-term effect is a buildup of carbon dioxide in the atmosphere, the so-called "greenhouse effect," which is even more difficult to analyze because the process proceeds so slowly. Carbon dioxide in the atmosphere reflects heat back down onto the earth's surface, stopping it from radiating out into space. If carbon dioxide in the atmosphere continues to build up at the present rate, the result, over the next century or so, could be an increase of 2 degrees to 8 degrees Fahrenheit in the temperature of air near the ground. A temperature increase of 3 degrees to 4 degrees Fahrenheit could change the world's climate enough to reduce the rainfall available in many parts of the world. An increase of 5 degrees to 7 degrees Fahrenheit could raise the global sea level nearly two feet.

The concentration of carbon dioxide in the atmosphere has risen about 14 percent since 1850. (It still constitutes only 0.03 percent of all the gases in the air.) The rate of increase is accelerating, and some of this increase has resulted from more widespread use of fossil fuels. On the other hand, a large fraction of the increase is probably due to deforestation, the cutting down of forests. Plants absorb carbon dioxide and produce oxygen. Cutting down forests reduces the rate at which carbon dioxide can be transformed into oxygen.

If carbon dioxide continues to build up in the atmosphere, it may eventually limit the amount of coal that can be used as fuel during the next century. Fortunately, most scientists believe there is still time to study the problem before taking drastic action. A report of the National Academy of Sciences concluded: "The very near future [twenty years or so] would be better spent improving our knowledge . . . than in changing fuel mix or use."

This new knowledge may eventually hasten the development of nuclear power and renewable energy sources—which do not produce carbon dioxide—as alternatives to the use of fossil fuels. Reliance on both nuclear power and renewable resources will have to increase, in any case, to augment fuels from the earth in supplying the world's growing need for energy.

CHAPTER 7

The Energy Future: Nuclear Power

Never was a new energy era launched so suddenly or with such a combination of fear and promise. The date was December 2, 1942. The group of forty-two scientists who gathered in a concrete squash court beneath the Stagg Field grandstand at the University of Chicago were about to perform one of history's most revolutionary experiments. The squash court contained four hundred tons of graphite in blocks stacked sixteen feet high, making a pile that was eight feet square at the base. Dispersed throughout the graphite pile were blocks of uranium. The scientists hoped the uranium would spontaneously begin to heat up with atomic energy as they withdrew control rods made of cadmium from the pile. The object of the experiment was to create the first nuclear reactor.

At a signal from Enrico Fermi, the director of the project, a scientist on the floor of the squash court began to slowly pull out the main control rod. The rest of the scientists watched from a balcony. One of them held an ax. If the pile of uranium began to overheat, he would use it to cut a rope tied to the balcony rail. This would drop other control rods farther into the pile. The control rods would reduce the number of atomic particles traversing the pile—in theory, slowing the reaction.

The main control rod rose higher. At a certain point, Fermi told his assistant to stop pulling. He made a quick calculation on his slide rule. Geiger counters measured an increasing stream of radiation in the room. Other instruments registered a steady rise in the temperature inside the graphite and uranium pile. The other scientists waited anxiously. Finally Fermi announced, "The reaction is self-sustaining."

Fusion energy may someday power spacecraft on journeys beyond the solar system (left), but its first uses will be on earth, perhaps by the decade of 2010.

Albert Einstein as a young man, about the time he began serious work on the theory of relativity that showed matter could be transformed into energy.

The experiment had been successful. Fermi gave an order to replace the main control rod and the pile began to cool down. Someone brought out a bottle of wine, and the scientists toasted their success. The atomic age had been born.

The atomic reaction that Fermi and the other scientists had witnessed proved that matter could be changed into energy. For nearly forty years, scientists had known that this was theoretically possible. But they didn't know how to go about making it happen. At first, the possibility was discussed only as an interesting speculation arising from the work of Albert Einstein. Later, the drive to develop atomic energy became part of a dedicated war effort *(see Glossary, Nuclear Energy)*.

In 1901, Albert Einstein took a position as clerk in the Bern, Switzerland, patent office. Einstein had been refused an academic position because of his mediocre school record. He had been rejected for military service because of flat feet and varicose veins. Einstein's work at the patent office was dull: he checked patent applications for technical accuracy. The job left him with a good deal of free time. He used this time and the hours away from his job to think about the nature of space and time. Sometime during this period he developed the theory of relativity, which concluded that matter and energy were interchangeable.

Scientists had long believed that light is carried by waves in a substance called ether, which filled all space. If this were true, the speed of light would vary depending on whether the earth was moving across a stream of light or parallel to it, just as the speed of a boat on a river may vary as the boat goes with the current or across it.

Einstein decided quite early—perhaps as young as the age of sixteen—that the speed of light should always be the same. This would be true no matter how fast the earth was moving or in what direction. In that case, there would be no such thing as *absolute* motion through space. There would only be the *relative* motion of the earth compared to other objects in the universe. And the idea of relative motion would mean that light was made up of pure energy, not of ripples or waves that traveled through some cosmic "ether." Building on this radical idea, Einstein showed that electromagnetic radiation, such as light, could be transformed into matter and vice versa. He published these ideas about relative motion, light, and energy in a scientific journal in 1905.

Testing Einstein's Ideas

Perhaps the ultimate test of Einstein's ideas was to observe an actual transformation of mass into energy. Many scientists thought that the radiation, or energy, given off by certain elements, such as radium, was a result of this transformation *(see Glossary, Radioactivity)*. But since the change took place inside the atom, it was difficult to observe. Among those who rejected the implications of Einstein's theory was one of the leading English physicists, Ernest Rutherford. In a 1933 lecture, Rutherford said: "The energy produced by the breaking down of the atom is a very poor kind of thing. Anyone who expects a source of power from the transformation of these atoms is talking moonshine."

One year later, a man who had read Rutherford's speech applied for a patent on a way to produce atomic energy—that is, to change matter into energy.

The man was Leo Szilard, a Hungarian teaching in Germany who had left for England when Hitler came to power earlier in 1933. As he reflected on Rutherford's speech, it occurred to Szilard that atomic energy could be released in a sustained way by setting off a "chain reaction." In this reaction, particles emitted by one atom would strike others, causing them to break apart and send out more particles. This idea—like so many others in atomic physics—was elegantly simple. But it was very difficult to put to a practical test. It also had an ominous implication: unless the chain reaction of atoms was controlled, an explosion like nothing the world had ever seen would result, as the uncontrolled reaction kept building up.

Experimenters around the world began searching for ways to set off a nuclear chain reaction. In 1934, Enrico Fermi, then in Italy, split an atomic nucleus—the dense center kernel of an atom—for the first time. But he was unable to determine just what had happened. As war clouds gathered over Europe and Hitler began to put his anti-Semitic ravings into practice, many eminent scientists, including Einstein and Fermi, left Europe for the United States. But Lise Meitner, a brilliant physicist who had been working at the Kaiser Wilhelm Institute in Berlin, fled to Sweden instead. Her role in the development of atomic energy was brief but critical.

In 1938, two leading physicists, Otto Hahn and Fritz Strassman, of the Kaiser Wilhelm Institute, repeated Fermi's experiment. They succeeded in splitting a uranium nucleus and produced a shower of atomic particles.

Again, the results of the experiment were hard to understand. The two wrote to Lise Meitner, who

Dana P. Mitchell, Enrico Fermi, and John R. Dunning at Columbia University in 1939 (top), discussing how to harness the energy released through the fission of an atomic nucleus (right). The answer came three years later when Fermi built the first atomic reactor.

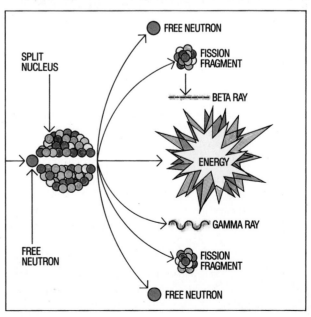

SPLIT NUCLEUS

FREE NEUTRON

FREE NEUTRON

FISSION FRAGMENT

BETA RAY

ENERGY

GAMMA RAY

FISSION FRAGMENT

FREE NEUTRON

The awesome power of nuclear energy is seen in this photograph of an atom bomb explosion during a 1957 test in the Nevada desert.

had worked with Hahn for many years, asking for her interpretation. On a long walk through the woods near Göteborg, Sweden, Meitner and her nephew, Otto Frisch, a physicist on vacation from his work in a laboratory in Denmark, suddenly understood what had happened: splitting the nucleus of the uranium atom represented the transformation of matter into energy. Frisch named the process of splitting "fission."

Back in Copenhagen, he told his boss, Niels Bohr, that atomic energy had finally been produced in the laboratory. Bohr was on his way to America. When he arrived, he conveyed the news to Szilard and Fermi, and the race to produce the atom bomb began. Beginning in 1940, the U.S. government launched a development effort of unprecedented magnitude. Called the Manhattan Project, its ultimate goal was to construct an atomic bomb.

Building the Bomb

A major problem was obtaining the right materials. In a chain reaction, neutrons (nuclear particles carrying no charge) from one fissioning nucleus must strike other nuclei before they escape.

Enough fissionable material must be brought together to form a critical mass—the amount of fissionable material necessary to spontaneously start a chain reaction. The chain reaction occurs and can be sustained because there are a sufficient number of neutrons colliding with fissionable nuclei.

The problem is that most of the uranium found in nature is uranium-238. The nucleus of a U-238 atom has 238 particles. In this type of uranium atom, the neutron does not cause fission. Instead it collides with the nuclei and is absorbed. Only one out of 140 uranium atoms found in nature has a fissionable nucleus, one with 235 particles. When a neutron collides with uranium-235 atoms, fission does occur.

Interestingly enough, when a uranium-238 atom absorbs a neutron, the atom then contains 239 nuclear particles and is transformed into plutonium. When another neutron strikes such a plutonium nucleus, fission can also occur.

This means there are at least two ways to produce fissionable material. The first is called enrichment. It involves increasing the concentration of uranium-235 atoms to a level above that found in natural uranium. During the Manhattan Project, uranium was enriched at Oak Ridge Laboratory in the mountains of eastern Tennessee.

Fermi's pile at the University of Chicago demonstrated that a nuclear chain reaction could be controlled and sustained. This made it possible to build special reactors that provided an alternative to the enrichment method in making fissionable materials. This second process, called transmutation, involves bombarding uranium-238 with neutrons inside a reactor and chemically separating out the plutonium that is produced. The transmutation process was accomplished at vast desert factories in Hanford, Washington, using pile-type reactors similar to the one Fermi used at the University of Chicago.

Once fissionable materials for the bomb were produced, they were carried to the secret mountaintop laboratory at Los Alamos, near Santa Fe, New Mexico. On the morning of July 16, 1945, at 5:29 A.M., the desert sky near Almagordo, New Mexico, flashed with a brilliance greater than midday. The first atomic bomb had exploded.

By this time, of course, Germany had surrendered. To end the war and save the lives of thousands of American and Allied soldiers, President Harry S Truman made the decision to detonate two atomic bombs over Japan. On August 14, 1945, Japan surrendered.

The Peaceful Uses of Nuclear Power

The same principles that govern the making of materials used in a bomb also apply to a nuclear reactor used to generate electricity. The purpose of such a reactor, of course, is not to create an explosive chain reaction, but rather to produce steam for electric generators. Fuel rods containing uranium are carefully spaced so that the neutrons produced by fissioning nuclei will hit enough other fissionable nuclei to sustain the chain reaction but not allow it to grow. A nuclear explosion in a power plant reactor cannot occur because the fissionable nuclei can never get close enough together to support an explosive chain reaction.

The reaction can be stopped at any time by using the control rods made of boron or cadmium that are placed in the spaces in between the fuel rods. The control rods control the speed of the chain reaction by absorbing neutrons. The farther the control rods are pushed into the reactor, the slower the nuclear reaction will become.

FOUR TYPES OF NUCLEAR REACTORS: Steam from the boiling water reactor (1) goes directly to drive a turbine to generate electricity. In a pressurized water reactor (2), water from the reactor core is pumped through a steam generator to release its heat. Similarly, blowers move gas through the core of a gas cooled reactor (3) and then into a steam generator. The liquid metal fast breeder reactor (4) uses molten sodium to cool the core, then two heat exchangers to provide steam to run a turbine.

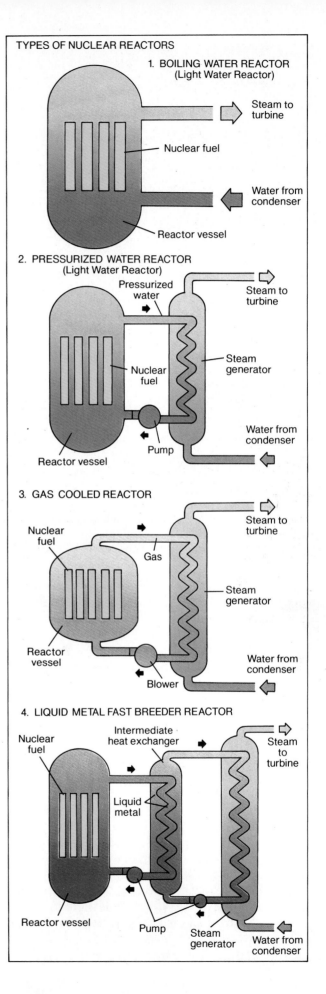

TYPES OF NUCLEAR REACTORS

1. BOILING WATER REACTOR
(Light Water Reactor)
Steam to turbine
Nuclear fuel
Water from condenser
Reactor vessel

2. PRESSURIZED WATER REACTOR
(Light Water Reactor)
Pressurized water
Steam to turbine
Nuclear fuel
Steam generator
Reactor vessel
Pump
Water from condenser

3. GAS COOLED REACTOR
Nuclear fuel
Gas
Steam to turbine
Steam generator
Reactor vessel
Blower
Water from condenser

4. LIQUID METAL FAST BREEDER REACTOR
Nuclear fuel
Intermediate heat exchanger
Steam to turbine
Liquid metal
Reactor vessel
Pump
Steam generator
Water from condenser

Light caused by the passage of radiation through water glows eerily from a research reactor at Oak Ridge National Laboratory in Tennessee.

When the rods are fully inserted, the chain reaction stops. But the fission by-products continue to produce heat. If they are not properly cooled, this heat can damage the reactor core, as was the case in the Three Mile Island accident.

After the war, graphite piles similar to Fermi's were adapted and used overseas to generate electricity. They were cooled by blowing air or carbon dioxide through the pile. This method of cooling was not efficient, however, and scientists began to consider using reactors cooled with water or molten sodium.

In 1947, the United States embarked on a national program to build nuclear submarines. By using a nuclear reactor to generate power for an electric motor propulsion system, submarines could operate almost indefinitely without refueling. The design chosen for this task was a light water reactor (LWR). It was so named because ordinary water was used to slow down the neutrons that passed among fuel rods. The water, under high pressure, also cooled the reactor and carried heat to the turbines, which drove the electric genera-

tors. This type of reactor required highly enriched uranium to make it compact enough for use on a submarine.

In 1948, Captain (later Admiral) Hyman G. Rickover, who led the Navy's nuclear sub program, confidently predicted that the first such submarine would be launched on January 1, 1955. Largely because of his tireless leadership, the USS *Nautilus* put to sea only seventeen days later than Rickover's target date.

The nuclear submarine program demonstrated the potential benefits of nuclear technology. Recognizing the need for the world to pursue the peaceful use of atomic energy, President Dwight D. Eisenhower on December 3, 1953, proposed his "Atoms for Peace" plan to the United Nations. This program initiated research that has resulted in the medical, agricultural, and industrial uses of nuclear technology, as well as its application in the production of electricity.

At the same time, the Atoms for Peace plan proposed the concept of safeguarding the use of nuclear materials and nuclear technology. Under the plan, a country that wants to receive nuclear materials and the know-how necessary to develop its own nuclear power program must agree to inspection of its nuclear facilities. The purpose of the inspection is to verify that the country is pursuing nuclear development for peaceful purposes only.

International control of nuclear weapons was furthered by the Nuclear Non-Proliferation Treaty. Countries signing this treaty do not have nuclear weapons programs, and they agree not to undertake the development of such nuclear devices. The first group of countries signed the treaty in 1968. By 1983, 119 countries had signed.

Largely because of the success of the reactors used in the nuclear submarine program, almost all of the more than eighty nuclear power plants operating in the United States today have light water reactors. As has been noted, the compact reactors on nuclear submarines use highly enriched uranium. In contrast, larger light water reactors in power plants use uranium enriched with from only 3 to 5 percent uranium-235. This makes these reactors both cheaper and safer.

Reactors that use slightly enriched uranium are much safer because the density of uranium-235 in these reactors is not great enough for an explosive chain reaction to occur. It is, in fact, physically impossible for a commercial light water reactor to explode like a bomb.

The water in a light water reactor serves another purpose in addition to cooling. A chain reaction cannot be sustained in commercial uranium fuel unless the fuel is submerged in water. When a uranium atom fissions and emits a neutron, the neutron is traveling very fast. It tends to ricochet off other uranium-235 atoms rather than split them. The neutrons are slowed down when the fuel is placed in water. These slower neutrons have a greater tendency to fission uranium-235 atoms, thus sustaining the chain reaction.

The First Commercial Reactors

Using light water reactors, the U.S. Atomic Energy Commission (AEC) and Duquesne Light Company began generating electricity for civilian use in 1957. This first installation, located at the Shippingport Atomic Power Station west of Pittsburgh, generated only sixty million watts of power, compared to more than a billion watts generated by some of today's large reactors. But it stimulated considerable interest among electric power utilities. During the next five years, four other utilities began using increasingly larger reactors.

Finally, in 1963, came the order for the first "commercial" nuclear power plant. This major installation was built by Jersey Central Power and Light Company for its 515-million-watt electrical facility at Oyster Creek, New Jersey, and began operating in 1969.

Soon utility companies throughout the country were turning to reactors. By early 1971, more than twenty nuclear power plants had been licensed to generate a total of more than eight billion watts of electricity, and an additional fifty-five plants with a combined capacity of forty-six billion watts were under construction.

But by the mid-1970s, problems began to develop. Some plants cost more than planned, and anti-nuclear groups expressed concern about reactor safety and the disposal of nuclear wastes.

Yet nuclear power might have been expected to gain in popularity after the oil crisis of the mid-1970s. Instead, several factors virtually halted utility company orders for new reactors.

One important reason for the turn from nuclear power was the slower rate of growth in the demand for electricity, caused by the recessions that followed the sharp oil price increases in 1973–74 and 1979. The inflationary spiral of the late 1970s and early 1980s also took its toll, increasing the costs of building plants. There were other problems as well. Delays occurred after the decision by federal and state governments to permit groups to intervene in the licensing process of individual plants. New government regulations and requirements for changes in plant design after the Three Mile Island accident also slowed construction time and increased costs.

As a result of these and other factors, no nuclear power plants have been ordered in the U.S. since 1978, and no new orders are expected for at least several more years. That does not mean that the United States no longer needs nuclear energy. About forty-eight nuclear plants are still under construction. The U.S. now gets roughly 13 percent of its electricity from atomic energy. That figure is expected to rise to 20 percent by the mid-1990s.

A Second Nuclear Era

Before utilities again begin to order new reactors, the nuclear power industry will have to restore public confidence in nuclear technology. This confidence received a severe shock on March 28, 1979. On that date, the number two reactor at Metropolitan Edison Company's Three Mile Island power station, near Harrisburg, Pennsylvania, broke down. The accident severely damaged the reactor and released a very small amount of short-lived radioactivity into the environment. A faulty valve in the cooling water system and mistakes made by the plant operators caused the fuel-containing "core" of the reactor to begin to overheat and deteriorate. It was feared by some that gases formed inside the reactor would explode or that the core would melt and penetrate to the bottom of the concrete containment building.

No one was hurt in the accident, and later analysis showed that neither a gas explosion nor penetration of the containment building floor would have occurred even if the cooling water had not been restored. But cleanup costs are estimated at more than $900 million.

Equally serious was the damage to public confidence in nuclear power. Memories of the accident will undoubtedly haunt the nuclear industry for years to come.

The towers of the Three Mile Island nuclear power plant stand as silent witnesses of the accident that crippled the plant's reactor.

The Three Mile Island accident has led electric utilities to take steps to increase reactor safety and public confidence in nuclear power. The utilities formed the Nuclear Safety Analysis Center (NSAC) in Palo Alto, California, to identify potential safety and operating problems and recommend solutions to these problems. They also established the Institute of Nuclear Power Operations in Atlanta, Georgia, to improve operator training. And through the Electric Power Research Institute in Palo Alto, they are financing research on improved reactor design.

One of the first priorities in preparing for a nuclear future is to provide for the long-term storage of highly radioactive atomic wastes. A uranium fuel rod that has been in a reactor about three years has used up most of its fissionable uranium-235 nuclei. The rod must then be removed. A constant stream of neutrons has bombarded the uranium-238 in the rod, forming plutonium. This plutonium can be removed chemically and used as fuel in other reactors. But such reprocessing of nuclear fuel is very controversial in the U.S. There is fear that the plutonium might be diverted to weapons production. (Reactor fuel rods cannot be used to make bombs.)

Whether or not useful plutonium is removed from the used fuel rods, the remaining radioactive waste material must be stored for a very long time. A few of the isotopes produced in a reactor remain radioactive for hundreds of thousands of years. The volume of such highly radioactive waste is not large. A billion-watt reactor produces only about two cubic meters of such waste each year. This volume is small enough to fit under a desk. The problem is where to store it so that no radioactivity harms the environment.

In the United States, the federal government has assumed responsibility for disposal of radioactive wastes. The Department of Energy is in the process of selecting a permanent repository site. Radioactive wastes will be stored deep underground in geologic formations which have been stable for millions of years.

The first repository is scheduled to start accepting radioactive materials in 1998. Current plans do not provide for reprocessing. Instead, used fuel assemblies will be placed in metal and concrete containers and buried deep underground in salt, granite, basalt, or volcanic rock formations. There are enough such sites in the United States to receive all the country's high-level wastes for the foreseeable future.

Experts believe a second nuclear era will begin when demand for electricity increases enough to make new power plants necessary. To launch this era, scientists are working on designs for safer, less expensive reactors. The cost of constructing new light water reactors could be reduced significantly by using standardized parts, rather than custom-building each plant, as has been the case.

Smaller LWR reactors might produce 500 or 600 million watts, rather than 1,000 to 1,200 million watts. They might also gain popularity because of their lower initial cost, reduced construction time, and greater flexibility in matching a utility's growth needs. To provide an extra margin of safety, a Swedish scientist has proposed building LWR reactors inside underground pools of water. The theory is that if something went wrong, cooling water would inundate the reactor.

Scientists are continuing to study and evaluate new types of reactors, always hopeful that an inexpensive fail-safe reactor can be produced.

By the next century, nuclear power plants will have used enough uranium to produce scarcity. Breeder reactors might then be needed to extend the supply of atomic fuel. A breeder reactor uses a mixture of plutonium and uranium-238 as fuel. Its fuel rods are surrounded by rods containing only uranium-238. Neutrons from the fissioning plutonium strike the uranium-238 nuclei and transform them into new plutonium. A breeder reactor produces more plutonium than will be consumed in the fuel rods, thus creating a supply of fissionable material. Over time, the use of breeder reactors to produce plutonium could increase the world's supply of nuclear fuel sixty-fold in comparison to the use of only uranium-235.

Today's breeder reactors are cooled by molten sodium flowing through pipes in the reactor core. This type of reactor is called a liquid metal fast breeder reactor (LMFBR). The United States pioneered development of LMFBRs in the 1950s,

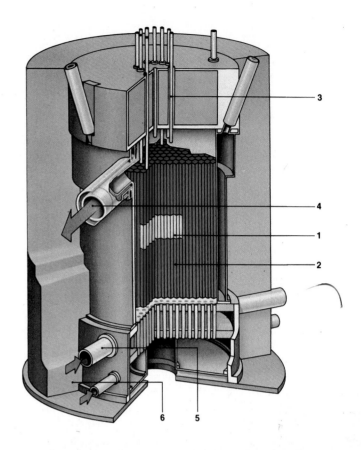

A breeder reactor produces more nuclear fuel than it consumes by changing the non-fuel uranium-238 into fissionable plutonium-239. Neutrons produced by fission of uranium-235 in the central part of the reactor core (1) spread out through the uranium-238 (2), which absorbs them and undergoes reactions that create new plutonium fuel. Boron control rods (3) are interspersed throughout the core. Liquid sodium coolant (4, 5) carries away the fission heat, which is used in a steam-driven electric generator. A concrete radiation shield (6) surrounds the reactor.

but further development has virtually ceased in this country. France now leads the world in breeder reactor research.

Producing a Fusion Reactor

Breeder reactors provide the prospect of an adequate supply of nuclear fuel far into the future. But the ultimate nuclear power source would use a virtually inexhaustible supply of fuel, in a fundamentally different type of atomic reaction. This reaction does not involve fission, the splitting of atomic nuclei, but rather fusion, the joining together of atomic nuclei. Fusion reactions are the source of energy that powers the sun. Fusion reactors would use atoms from heavy water as fuel.

Heavy water exists in sea water and can be separated from it. Hydrogen atoms in heavy water have an extra neutron in their nuclei. The hydrogen atoms of heavy water undergo fusion if they are brought together under great pressure and at high temperatures. This fusion releases enormous amounts of energy.

Unfortunately, the necessary conditions of high temperature and great pressure are very hard to achieve simultaneously. This explains why fusion reactors are not already generating power. So far, fusion takes place only in experimental machines that use up much more energy than they produce.

Reaching energy break-even—the point at which as much energy is produced as is used up —presents a substantial scientific challenge. Nuclei of heavy hydrogen must be heated to 100 million degrees Centigrade and confined, so that more than 100,000 billion of them occupy one cubic centimeter (about the size of a sugar cube).

Scientists are now concentrating on two basic ways of bringing this about. The leading method is called magnetic confinement. It involves creating enormously powerful magnetic fields that squeeze heavy hydrogen nuclei together. The most advanced magnetic confinement machine is the Tokamak. (This Russian word stands for "toroidal magnetic chamber.") In the Tokamak, nuclei are held in a toroidal, or doughnut-shaped, magnetic field. The nuclei are squeezed into a "plasma," a gas composed of atoms that have been stripped of their electrons.

The largest American Tokamak, called the Tokamak Fusion Test Reactor (TFTR), went into operation in December 1982 at the Princeton Plasma Physics Laboratory in Princeton, New Jersey. The plasma in the TFTR is confined in an evacuated toroidal vessel more than twenty-one feet in diameter and more than six feet high.

An alternative design for magnetic confinement holds a plasma between two magnetic "mirrors," which reflect escaping charged particles in the plasma to confine them. The largest of these machines in the United States is called the Mirror Fusion Test Facility B (MFTF-B). It is scheduled to begin operation at the Lawrence Livermore National Laboratory near San Francisco in 1986.

The second method for producing fusion is called inertial confinement. It involves bombarding small pellets of heavy hydrogen with either lasers or beams of charged particles—for example, heavy ions, which are electrically charged atoms. The world's largest laser, the SHIVA laser, is capable of focusing 10,000 joules of energy almost instantaneously onto a pellet of heavy hydrogen. The SHIVA is now being used to conduct inertial confinement fusion experiments at Lawrence Livermore National Laboratory. So far, SHIVA research has provided much new data. But scientists need to continue their developmental work on the concept of bombardment by lasers. They are planning to build a 300,000-joule laser, called NOVA, for use in the late 1980s.

The technology that would permit beams of charged particles to be aimed toward a fusion fuel pellet is not as far advanced as that involving lasers. But this alternative approach might ultimately work better. A reactor using particle beams might produce 100 million watts of electric power from a reactor chamber only nine feet in diameter.

Experimental fusion devices are expected to achieve scientific energy break-even before the end of the 1980s. But "scientific energy break-even" means that many years of further engineering development will be needed before commercial fusion reactors begin producing substantial amounts of electric power. The United States Department of Energy estimates that the first fusion power reactor may be built sometime between the turn of the century and the year 2010. Commercial demonstration of the technology would follow perhaps a decade later.

Fusion power would provide the world with a virtually inexhaustible supply of energy. The radioactive materials produced by a fusion reactor would be easier to deal with than those created by a fission reactor. But fusion reactors would not be perfectly clean sources of energy. Metals used in the interiors of such reactors would become extremely radioactive and would have to be disposed of when the reactor was dismantled at the end of its life. As promising as the fusion reactor seems to be, many such considerations need to be dealt with before the advent of fusion power.

Future Energy Needs

Nuclear power is of course used mainly to produce electricity, which is perhaps the most versatile form of energy. Its great virtue is that it can be generated from many primary sources of energy, ranging from nuclear energy, oil, and coal to renewable resources such as water, wind, solar, and geothermal energy. For generating electricity, coal and uranium are both much cheaper fuels than oil or gas—and they are much more plentiful.

To supply our energy needs as we move into the twenty-first century, we must rely on a combination of the energy sources that are already available, primarily oil, coal, and nuclear fission power. And we must use these sources for their highest-priority purposes. For this reason, oil will continue to be used primarily for transportation. Its use to generate electricity will decline, and the use of coal, uranium, and various renewable resources will increase.

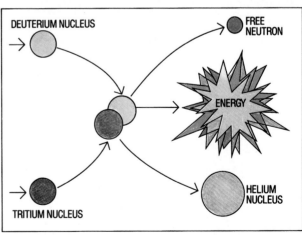

Fusion energy, which is released when nuclei of deuterium and tritium join to form helium, may someday provide an alternative to fission energy. Above, Harold Furth, director of the Princeton Plasma Physics Laboratory, stands before the lab's Tokamak Fusion Test Reactor.

CHAPTER 8

The Energy Future: Sun, Wind, and Water

Energy resources such as fossil fuels and uranium must be discovered and extracted from beneath the earth. Their supply is limited. But there are other energy resources that are "renewable." Because they are produced naturally, their supply can continue indefinitely. Solar energy becomes available with every sunrise. Rain replenishes the rivers and lakes that provide hydroelectric power. Winds howl through mountain passes with such regularity that wind turbines can be counted on to generate electricity almost every day. Geothermal heat rises from magma, or molten earth, that continually pushes up close to the earth's surface. It provides energy through steam and hot water. Some fuels may also be considered to be renewable. Supplies of firewood and garbage, for instance, will remain steady as long as forests and municipal wastes are well managed.

Although renewable resources are available virtually forever, many problems prevent their wider use. The main problem is cost. Extracting useful heat from sunlight or converting it into electricity, for example, requires large, expensive collectors. In addition, some regions have less sunlight than others. Also, harnessing most renewable resources for their maximum potential depends on further technological development. Wind turbines need improvements in cost and reliability if they are to compete with fossil fuels in generating electricity. Other systems for utilizing renewable resources on a large scale require the invention of radically new technology.

In spite of such difficulties, the prospects for wider use of renewable energy resources are bright. The price of fossil fuels will continue to rise. Users must pay the cost of controlling the pollution sometimes created by these fuels, while cleaner alternatives such as solar power and wind do not present this problem. At the same time, new technology will help to reduce the price of

Hydroelectric power, like that produced at Chief Joseph Dam in Washington, is likely to remain the most important source of renewable energy for decades.

energy from some renewable resources and make others easier to use. Still, renewable energy resources will contribute less to America's total energy needs than oil, coal, and nuclear power well into the twenty-first century.

Of all renewable energy resources used in the U.S., hydroelectric power—electricity generated by water-driven turbines—has, since the 1930s, remained by far the most important. It was during the thirties that great dams were built across major waterways throughout the country, with the result that almost 40 percent of U.S. electricity was generated by hydroelectric facilities. Today, water power still accounts for 12 percent of America's total electric energy and for 98 percent of the electricity generated from renewable resources.

The growth of hydroelectric power has slowed considerably during the last several decades. The primary reason is that many of the most promising sites for dams are already being used. The Columbia River system alone has 192 dams. These produce electricity at rates that are less than half the cost of power in other parts of the country. Now scientists are re-examining such dams to see if they can generate even more power. New dams are being planned for smaller rivers, which were once considered incapable of generating enough power to merit their use.

There are a number of ways to increase the output of electricity at present dams. At some sites, engineers can add more generators. At others, reservoir levels can be raised and generators improved. Spillway gates can also be designed to reduce the waste of water during periods of heavy rainfall. Improved maintenance of equipment can play an important role as well. Proper maintenance can reduce the time a generator is unavailable to produce electricity. Raising the average time that equipment is available at U.S. hydroelectric plants by just 1 percent represents a savings to utilities of $150 million a year.

Building a new generation of smaller, less powerful hydroelectric facilities is more complicated than upgrading older power plants. Large dams may be several hundred feet high. This means that the water pressure near their base is powerful enough to run very large turbines and generate

several million kilowatts of electricity. Small hydroelectric facilities usually have water heights of only twenty to sixty-five feet. They can generate less than twenty thousand kilowatts of power. Such facilities are too small to justify the construction of customized power-generating equipment. New kinds of standardized equipment will be needed to make practical the development of many small hydroelectric sites.

The amount of power available from hydroelectric plants in the United States is expected to increase more than 50 percent by the year 2000. To achieve this growth, environmental problems at each new dam site will have to be overcome. Changes in reservoir water levels, for example, can seriously affect plants along the shoreline. Dams can interfere with fish migration. And hydroelectric plants can sharply lower downstream water temperatures when cold water drawn from the bottom of dams passes through the generators, is released, and flows downstream. Environmental effects such as these can be minimized. If the licensing of new dams can be speeded up, hydroelectric power will remain the largest source of renewable energy well into the next century.

Advanced Solar Energy Technology

Next to hydroelectric power, the most promising renewable energy resource is solar energy. The availability of advanced techniques and devices to harness sunlight now provides new opportunities for the development of solar power. Three areas of innovation show particular promise: new ways to heat and cool homes with solar energy; the use of focused sunlight to create steam for generating electricity; and the direct conversion, using solar cells, of light into electric power.

Heating and Cooling Homes. The simplest way to heat a home using solar energy is to build large windows facing south to catch sunlight and let the light fall on special heat-absorbing walls. Covering the windows with a thin glaze helps hold the heat inside. Window blinds and movable slabs of insulation can be used to control the amount of heat let in. Air ducts and fans circulate the air to keep the house temperature uniform.

This is known as a "passive" solar heating system. Such a system must usually be built into new homes, and it can add substantially to the cost of a house.

"Active" solar heating systems use panels of black metal or plastic to absorb the sun's heat. Water circulates through the panels and transfers heat into the house through pipes. The heat is stored in the house, usually in a tank of hot water, so that it can be made available after sundown. To

By reflecting the sun's rays on a small area, the solar furnace at Odeillo, France (right) can produce temperatures of 3,800 Centigrade. Below, solar panels provide heat for a building in Huntsville, Alabama.

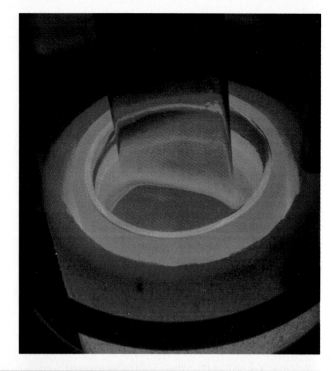

warm the house, a fan blows room air over thin metal vanes in a unit attached to pipes through which hot water is pumped from the storage tank, creating a supply of hot air.

Most active solar heating systems require backup heaters that run on natural gas or electricity. The backup system provides heat on cloudy days and unusually cold nights. A backup heater adds to the initial cost of the system. But reduced fuel bills help offset the initial cost.

One of the most energy-efficient ways to both heat and cool a house is to use an electric heat pump in combination with solar collectors and storage tanks. The heat pump works like a refrigerator—cooling the air in a room by transferring heat from the room to the outside. Such combined solar/heat pump systems are now being studied by utilities to determine in which part of the country they might prove most economical.

About 25 percent of U.S. energy is expended in heating and cooling buildings. The use of more solar heating and cooling systems can help cut this amount by as much as 10 percent, thus reducing dependence on fossil fuels.

Generating Electricity from Solar Heat. In the desert of southern California, about twelve miles southeast of Barstow, an imposing steel tower rises 310 feet into the air. Spread out around it, covering 130 acres, are 1,818 mirrors mounted on poles. A motor controls each mirror, rotating it so that the mirror reflects the sun's light toward the top of the tower in order to heat water in a tank. A computer synchronizes the motors so that the mirrors continuously track the sun as it moves across the sky. The reflected sunlight boils water that is used to generate ten thousand kilowatts of electricity, using an ordinary steam turbine.

This is Solar One, the first power plant in the United States that generates large amounts of electricity from sunlight. The plant cost more than

Solar photovoltaic cells (left) convert sunlight directly into electricity. At present, they are expensive and not widely used. To lower costs, new ways are being developed to manufacture them. One experimental method, shown above, produces thin, flat sheets of silicon for use in solar cells.

$21 million and began operating in 1982. Southern California Edison Company owns Solar One, which on a sunny day provides enough electricity to meet the needs of seven thousand to ten thousand people. Heat stored in a sixty-foot-wide tank provides enough steam to operate the turbines without sunlight for about four hours.

The main purpose of this new facility is to provide utilities with firsthand experience in operating a solar power generator. If tests at Solar One prove successful, the next plants built may be three to ten times as large. They may also use gas turbines rather than steam turbines. In that case, heat from the sun would expand a gas, such as helium, in order to drive the turbine during the day. At night, natural gas could be burned to drive the same turbine. Such a hybrid arrangement makes more efficient use of both sunlight and equipment.

Other designs may also be used to generate electricity from solar heat. The Solar One design is an example of a "power tower," in which the boiler sits on top of a high tower and receives light from many movable flat mirrors near the ground. A much smaller device could be made, using a single large parabolic mirror to focus light onto a boiler mounted only a few feet away. Another alternative is to build long troughs lined with reflective material. The troughs concentrate light onto a water pipe suspended above them. This system operates at a lower temperature than the power tower or parabolic mirror designs, but it could be used to produce heat and electric power to run a factory.

Electricity from Solar Cells. Electricity can be generated from the sun's light without focusing heat onto a boiler to create steam. The advantage of such a system of photovoltaic, or solar, cells is that they do not require large mechanical generators or movable mirrors to track the sun. The disadvantage is that the silicon cells in the system are expensive and can convert only small amounts of light energy at a time into electrical energy.

Albert Einstein first explained the principle on which photovoltaic cells work in one of his many contributions to modern science—the one for which he won the 1921 Nobel physics prize. Scientists had long known that when light falls on certain materials, including silicon, electrons are knocked loose. What they did not understand was why the energy of these electrons should depend on the *color* of the light.

Einstein proved that light travels in little bundles of energy, later called "photons." The amount of energy a photon has is governed by its wavelength, which in turn determines its color. When a photon strikes an electron in just the right way, it displaces that electron from its orbit around the nucleus of the atom. Photons with certain colors (such as blue) have more energy than those of other colors (such as red). An electron that absorbs a photon of blue light moves faster than one that absorbs a photon of red light.

A photovoltaic cell uses this principle. The cell consists of two thin layers of silicon. One layer has been made more attractive to electrons than the other. As sunlight strikes the silicon, photons of certain colors displace electrons. The displaced electrons then collect in one of the layers, and electricity flows through a wire leading from the electron-rich layer to the electron-poor layer. A small photovoltaic cell generates only enough electricity to run a digital watch or a pocket calculator. By connecting many thousands of such cells, several kilowatts of power can be generated.

Raw silicon is quite cheap—it can be found in ordinary sand. But extremely precise and expensive manufacturing steps are required to prepare the silicon for use in photovoltaic cells. Scientists have still not determined the best of several possible ways to build the cells. They are concerned most of all about the trade-off between the cost of a cell and the efficiency with which it transforms solar energy into electric energy. Cells made from large single crystals of silicon are the most efficient but also the most expensive. Cells made from noncrystalline silicon cost less but don't work as well. Electricity generated by today's commercial photovoltaic cells still costs about ten times as much as that available through utility power lines.

Despite their relatively high cost, solar cells are gaining in popularity. They are used in remote areas not reached by power lines to provide electricity for communications facilities, irrigation pumps, scientific research stations, and an esti-

Windmills with giant airplane-type propellers are becoming familiar sights in coastal regions. One day they may be erected offshore (above).

mated ten thousand isolated homes. Such applications offer particular advantages in developing countries. Three remote villages in the Saudi Arabian desert, for instance, have been receiving power from a 350-kilowatt photovoltaic power plant since 1982. In the United States, the first privately funded photovoltaic power plant was built in 1983. It now provides one thousand kilowatts of power to the Southern California Edison Company. (A major coal or nuclear power plant generates one million or more kilowatts of power.)

As the cost of solar cells continues to fall, larger and more numerous power plants can be built. A private company is also building a 16,500-kilowatt photovoltaic power plant in northern California, scheduled for partial operation in 1984. The Pacific Gas and Electric Company will buy the electricity from this plant. The Sacramento Municipal Utility District has begun work on what would be the world's largest photovoltaic facility—a one hundred thousand-kilowatt plant to be completed by 1994. Clearly, the use of photovoltaic cells will continue to increase. The rate of growth in their manufacture is now nearly 75 percent a year.

However, even the most optimistic projections show photovoltaic electricity contributing less than 1 percent of the total generating capacity of the United States by the turn of the century.

Energy from the Wind

By the end of the nineteenth century, around 6.5 million windmills supplied mechanical energy to pump water and grind grain on farms throughout the United States. Wind power proved as vital to farmers settling frontier lands as it was to sailors carrying their goods to distant lands. Now a new generation of wind machines is being developed to meet the energy needs of the late twentieth century. Generating electric power for isolated farms or for distribution through utility power lines, these new wind turbines can already be seen swinging their great arms on top of windy hills or facing ocean breezes.

These giant machines are a far cry from the small clanking windmills that still pump water on many farms. Most wind turbines have only two blades, shaped like those on an airplane propeller but large enough to span a football field if laid on the ground. Some of the biggest generate as much as five thousand kilowatts of power— enough to supply the needs of more than one thousand homes. The state of California has the country's most aggressive program to develop wind power. At the end of 1983, there were more than 4,600 electricity-generating wind turbines operating in California, and they were capable of producing a total of about three hundred thousand kilowatts of electricity.

The National Aeronautics and Space Administration (NASA) has managed technological development of some of the most advanced power-producing wind turbines. These are designed to be very tall. Their height lets them take advantage of stronger winds and use very long blades for greater power-generating capacity. One of the most advanced models is called the MOD-2 design. Three wind turbines built with this design now operate near Goldendale, Washington. There are similar units near Medicine Bow, Wyoming, and in Solano County, California. Each unit consists of a tower two hundred feet high, with rotor blades 150 feet long. A MOD-2 unit can generate 2,500 kilowatts of power if the wind is blowing at about twenty-eight miles per hour. Winds of less than fourteen miles per hour are too weak for generating power in a MOD-2. The unit shuts down automatically at forty-five miles per hour to prevent damage.

More radical designs are also being tested. One of these, invented in the 1930s by a Frenchman, G. J. M. Darrieus, consists of thin blades anchored at top and bottom on a vertical axle. It looks something like an overgrown eggbeater. Such a design has several advantages. Using the Darrieus wind machine, heavy electrical generating equipment can be put on the ground rather than supported on top of a large tower, as is the case with propeller-blade wind turbines. And the vertical blades of a Darrieus wind machine can easily accept wind from any direction. Propeller-blade turbines, in contrast, have to be rotated so that their propellers always face directly into the wind. But the Darrieus design is less efficient than propeller-type wind machines at converting wind energy into electrical energy. Sandia Laboratories, in Albuquerque, New Mexico, now manages development of Darrieus machines for the U.S. Department of Energy and has built a few small prototypes.

Wind turbines now come close to competing economically with oil-fired power plants for generating electricity in some parts of the United States.

Further technological development will bring the cost down even further. But more research is needed to remedy safety and mechanical problems that have sometimes plagued the new wind turbines. One five hundred-kilowatt machine in southern California collapsed entirely after a rotor malfunction. And one of the three MOD-2 units in Washington state began running too fast and damaged its generator.

Even with improved technology, wind energy has limitations. Many of the windiest areas of the country, which could provide ideal sites for wind turbines, are far from the urban areas that most need electric power. Ecological concerns may prevent the construction of wind turbines in other promising areas. For example, scientists have yet

A Darrieus windmill has a vertical axis that accepts wind from any direction; the design allows the heavy generating equipment to be placed on the ground.

to determine exactly what effect giant moving blades can have on weather patterns, bird migrations, and air navigation. Finally, in most places not enough land may be available to build a sufficient number of wind turbines. Clusters of these devices require four or five times as much land as solar power installations to generate the same amount of electricity.

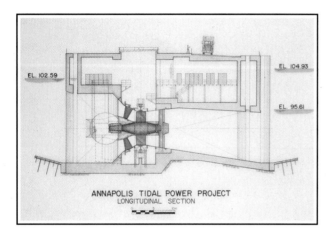

EL. 102.59

EL. 104.93

EL. 95.61

ANNAPOLIS TIDAL POWER PROJECT
LONGITUDINAL SECTION

The Annapolis Tidal Power Project will generate electricity from the movement of tides through a turbine built into a dam across the narrow opening to Annapolis Basin, off the Bay of Fundy in Canada.

Energy from the Earth

Ninety miles north of San Francisco at The Geysers, steam has vented for centuries from cracks in the earth. This steam now provides heat to run turbines at the largest geothermal power source in the United States. The turbine generates about one million kilowatts of electricity. By 1990, the Pacific Gas and Electric Company plans to expand generating capacity at the site to nearly two million kilowatts.

Regions with this type of "dry steam" coming from the ground are very rare—representing only about one-half of 1 percent of all U.S. geothermal resources. Perhaps two dozen states, however, have hydrothermal (or underground hot water) resources. A major research effort is now under way to identify these untapped resources and to develop the technology to use them.

This photo of workmen on the turbine generator at the Annapolis project shows the enormous size of equipment needed to extract energy from tides.

Where geothermal hot water occurs underground at temperatures above 210 degrees Centigrade, a "direct flash" technology can be used to generate electricity. When this water is brought to the surface, it undergoes a drop in pressure which allows it to boil. The steam produced can be used to drive a turbine. The first experimental plant using this direct-flash method to extract energy from an underground reservoir of hot water began operating in 1980 at Brawley, California. The plant generates ten thousand kilowatts of electricity for the Southern California Edison Company and the Union Oil Company of California.

A more complex approach is needed when the temperature or pressure of underground hot water is too low for it to boil when brought to the surface. In this case, another liquid with a much lower boiling temperature than water is used to absorb heat from the geothermal water. The second liquid then vaporizes and drives a turbine. The first geothermal power plant to use this binary cycle design, as it is called, is scheduled to begin generating power in late 1984 at Heber, California, near the Mexican border. The plant will generate forty-five thousand kilowatts of electric power. It is expected to cost a total of $122 million to build and operate for a two-year demonstration period. If this demonstration is successful, binary cycle

plants may be used commercially in other parts of the country as early as 1986.

With new technology, geothermal resources could contribute substantially to America's energy needs. Some experts estimate that geothermal plants with a capacity to generate twenty-four million kilowatts could be built during the next twenty years. This would make geothermal energy second only to hydroelectric power among renewable resources.

Energy from Wood and Refuse

India and the United States now use about equal amounts of wood for fuel—130 million tons. That represents about 3 percent of America's energy needs and one-fourth of India's. The uses of firewood in each country differ as well. In India it is a necessity of daily life—the poor man's major fuel, used for cooking and heating. In the United States, the re-emergence of firewood as a fuel has to do with a need to use every form of energy available. Many homeowners burn available wood to lower heating fuel bills, and some factories are taking advantage of wood scrap that previously was wasted. The forest products industry now supplies about half of its own energy needs by burning its own wood scrap.

New technology is also helping. Some of today's wood-burning stoves are much more efficient than those used a couple of generations ago. Chipping machines can reduce a whole tree into small and easily used pieces. Special pollution control equipment has been developed to reduce the spread of toxic materials in wood smoke. In addition to trees, smaller plants like the creosote bush, which will grow in poor soil under dry conditions, are being considered as sources of "biomass," biological materials that can be used as fuel. The important point is that these materials do not replace crops. They can be grown economically on otherwise unproductive land.

Dozens of communities around the country have also begun to burn municipal waste to produce steam for local industries or to generate a local supply of electricity. Americans produce about 150 million tons of such refuse each year, and scientists are actively seeking ways to extract energy from it in an economical way.

As new ways to burn wood and waste are developed, communities, factories, and electrical utilities will increase their use of these most readily available fuels.

Experimental Sources of Energy

Three other, more speculative sources of renewable energy have also attracted scientists' attention during the last decade: tidal energy, ocean heat, and power from outer space. So far, there has been one big obstacle to harnessing these resources—the cost of building the equipment.

Of the three, only tidal energy has actually been used to generate electricity commercially. In 1966,

a tidal power plant was built on the Rance River in Brittany, France. This plant still uses the daily movement of tides to run twenty-four turbines installed near the river mouth. Although the plant can generate 240,000 kilowatts of power at peak water flow, it operates only about one-fourth of the time because of changing currents. Few other places in the world have tidal water movements with even this potential for producing energy. Perhaps the most promising site is Passamaquoddy Bay, an arm of the Bay of Fundy between Maine and New Brunswick, Canada. But it may be extremely difficult to raise the billions of dollars required to build a dam across this vast stretch of

---

Steam rises from a geothermal energy installation in Iceland, which has more natural hot springs and steam geysers than any other country in the world.

Power plants may someday grow their own fuel. Here, a harvesting machine is cutting trees and separating the wood that would be burned to produce electricity.

swiftly moving water. And the environmental effects of such a dam would have to be carefully considered.

In 1984, construction was winding up on a twenty-megawatt tidal power station that dams up Annapolis Basin, a small bay off the Bay of Fundy. At high tide, water that once flowed into the bay now flows through turbines to generate electricity that helps fill the energy needs of about five to ten thousand households. Because the opening of the basin is quite small, this power station will cost only a fraction of the amount that would be required to dam up larger areas of the Bay of Fundy.

Producing energy by using the heat of the ocean also involves the problem of high cost. Ocean-thermal energy conversion (OTEC) systems generate electricity by using the temperature differences that exist between the warmer surface waters and the colder depths of tropical oceans *(see Glossary, Ocean-Thermal Energy Conversion).* The system vaporizes liquid ammonia with warm surface water. This causes the ammonia to expand and drive a turbine. The ammonia is then condensed back into a liquid by cooling it with water pumped up from below. Instead of burning fuel, OTEC systems produce electricity by using energy that exists in ocean waters.

But the energy-saving advantages of OTEC systems are offset by their great cost. Even a modest-size OTEC power plant, with only one-tenth the generating capacity of many coal or nuclear facilities, would require an enormous investment. Such a plant would have a flow of water comparable to that of Boulder Dam.

Using power from space also presents problems of cost. Some scientists have suggested that energy in the form of microwaves could be beamed to earth from solar-powered satellites. But to do this, a satellite capable of transmitting less than one-tenth the power of an ordinary coal-fired plant would have to contain roughly twenty square miles of photovoltaic cells. And it would have to beam its power to a thirty-acre receiving station on earth. Each satellite and receiving station would cost from $10 to $20 billion. There are also serious questions about the environmental effects of such a system. Microwaves of the necessary intensity might harm plants, animals, or humans that came within range of the giant beam.

As this survey indicates, renewable resources will play an important role in the future of energy development. But each type has limitations that are imposed by nature. Some of these resources, including hydroelectric power and geothermal energy, already represent economically attractive alternatives to coal and nuclear power—where they are available. Others, such as photovoltaic cells and wind turbines, require further technological development before they can achieve general commercial success, and some, such as solar satellites, may seem to be theoretically attractive, but they probably would cost too much to become a reality.

CHAPTER **9**

The Coming Energy Transition

The Eiffel Tower, completed in 1889, quickly became a leading symbol of late nineteenth-century technology. Rising 984 feet into the air in the center of the city of Paris, the tower was considered a marvel of engineering. Even today it dominates the Parisian skyline.

By contrast, some of the most spectacular engineering marvels of the late twentieth century will be all but invisible to most people. They are the giant offshore oil platforms that already rise as high as one thousand feet from the ocean floor and stand firmly enough to withstand one-hundred-foot waves. Such platforms make an appropriate symbol of technology for the present age, which must achieve a transition to a more stable energy future.

The size and cost—billions of dollars in some cases—of the ocean platforms now under construction point up both the increasing difficulty of obtaining energy and the high value of the world's remaining oil resources. When the Statfjord B platform was towed one hundred miles into the North Sea from a construction site in Norway in 1981, it became the heaviest object ever moved by man. Weighing almost nine hundred thousand tons while being towed, the Statfjord B was one hundred times heavier than the Eiffel Tower.

From such platforms—and from other massive drilling projects—will come the oil needed to keep cars running and homes heated until additional energy resources can be developed. Such additional sources are already being used. About 10 percent of the oil now consumed in the United States, for example, goes to heat homes and businesses. This share is expected to fall by half, to about 5 percent, by the year 2000. Electric heat pumps, gas furnaces, and solar energy systems will increasingly replace oil-fired units for this purpose. At the same time, however, the demand for oil in industry is expected to grow, and transportation will continue to depend primarily on oil.

With the dawn of the 21st century will come new attitudes toward energy. The passengers on Spaceship Earth may look toward outer space for help in achieving energy stability at home. At left, a solar power station helps support the space shuttle on long-duration flights of up to 120 days.

As easily accessible deposits of petroleum diminish, more exploration will be conducted in remote areas. The rig above is in the North Sea.

A Complex Transition

As this overview indicates, the coming energy transition will be quite complex. It will involve making many different energy choices throughout society. Exactly how much energy will come from each source at any particular time in the future is very hard to predict.

Nevertheless, some overall trends are already becoming evident. These trends involve four main elements: the supply of particular energy sources, the cost of using them, the development of new technologies, and the effects of government policies. The importance of these considerations in the changing picture of American and world en-

ergy supply and demand can best be understood by examining the major future sources of energy.

Petroleum. Oil is expected to remain the single largest U.S. energy source for the remainder of this century. The demand for this vital resource peaked in the late 1970s. It will probably remain fairly constant until sometime after the year 2000. The main reason oil will remain so important is that it offers unique advantages as a fuel for many uses. Petroleum products have a high heat content, they are easy to transport and store, and they can release energy in a variety of engines, ranging from single-cylinder lawn mowers to the giant turbines that drive electric generators.

As oil becomes more expensive, we can expect to see its use concentrated more and more in those areas where it is most valuable. In other words, cars will burn oil far into the twenty-first century. So will remote factories to which oil can be transported more easily than other fuels. Electric power plants and home furnaces will probably be converted to less valuable energy sources.

The world is not "running out of oil." But new oil fields are increasingly hard to find and develop. Worldwide production has outpaced new discoveries since the early 1970s. Estimates of future discoveries indicate that global production will peak sometime after the year 2000. Just how soon this inevitable point of decline will be reached depends mainly on two considerations. The first is cost. What price are consumers willing to pay for this energy source as its declining supply makes it more expensive? And what will be the impact of new technologies—such as the giant offshore platforms—on the production of petroleum?

The major U.S. onshore oil fields have been producing for a long time and have begun to run down. Demand for oil will have to be met increasingly from remote areas—such as the northern part of Alaska, offshore in the Gulf of Mexico, and off the Pacific Coast where oil deposits are found on the outer continental shelf—and from imports. The amount of oil produced from new fields in remote areas will depend mainly on the cost of exploration. As domestic petroleum resources become more limited, the amount of imported oil the United States uses is expected to rise from the present level of 30 percent of the total to perhaps 55 percent by the year 2000.

Synthetic fuels represent another potential source of oil. But the timing for their development is difficult to project. Their price and their availability will depend on the success of new technology in developing the efficient and economic processes required to convert resources such as coal and oil shale into viable liquid and gaseous fuels.

In any event, synthetic fuels will not make a large contribution to the total energy supply until after the turn of the century.

Natural gas. During the next century, natural gas production will also be limited by declining resources. But for the present, new deposits are being discovered around the world faster than old ones are being consumed. Estimates of potential discoveries indicate that global production of natural gas could increase for at least the rest of this century. In the United States, however, production has been declining since about 1973. Gas imports may double by the year 2000. Even so, natural gas is expected to represent less than 20 percent of U.S. energy supply at that time, down from about 28 percent now.

Until new gas discoveries decline worldwide, the demand will be limited primarily by cost. Increasingly, new gas will come from very deep wells (those more than fifteen thousand feet in depth) and from offshore platforms, and this will make natural gas more expensive.

The success of new technology will also influence gas use. Cogeneration technology is one example. This is the burning of natural gas for an industrial process while generating electricity as well. By the year 2000, cogeneration may account for as much electric power production as fifty nuclear plants, if further technological development to reduce its cost is successful. Gas produced from coal may also become economically attractive for the generation of electricity by the turn of

the century—again depending on further technological development.

Coal. Most of the energy growth that takes place over the next several decades—both in the United States and the world at large—will come from coal. The 1980 World Coal Study report concluded that two-thirds of the world's energy growth for the rest of this century *could* come from coal, and at least one-half *must* come from coal. According to the study, both the money and the technology are available to increase coal production to a level that would fulfill these needs.

Coal supplies may be assured, but there are unanswered questions about how to burn coal without harming the environment. More scientific research will be needed to explore this issue. At the same time, scientists will continue to work on new technology to eliminate any adverse effects the use of coal has on the environment.

Water power may someday be harnessed by long lines of floating vanes moored offshore to rise and fall with passing waves, thereby generating electricity.

Future space colonies will have to be energy self-sufficient. Here, large rectangular mirrors direct solar energy into the interior of a colony.

Nuclear energy. Public opinion, government policies, economic uncertainties, and technological development are more intertwined for nuclear power than for any other source of energy. Those who favor nuclear energy declare that there is a clear need for reactors. The Electric Power Research Institute forecasts a bleak picture if construction of new nuclear power plants is limited to those currently under construction or on order. In that case, says the institute, the United States could experience shortages of electric power that would begin in the late 1980s. By the year 2010, this shortage could amount to more than 20 percent of needed generating capacity.

But the problems surrounding nuclear power represent a serious obstacle to future development. Construction of new plants is being delayed, costs are rising, and public confidence remains uncertain.

Perhaps the best vision of what a nuclear future might look like comes from France. That country made an all-out commitment to atomic energy in the early 1970s. France standardized design of the pressurized light water reactor, centralized production of major components, and coordinated a continuous, nationwide construction program. The French can build a new plant in less than six years—compared to about thirteen years in the United States. This approach has also kept costs down.

America certainly has the capacity to organize its nuclear program along the lines of the French approach. But this would require sorting out the present tangled lines of nuclear policy. To do so, we must resolve the sometimes conflicting demands of safety, reactor design, energy supply and demand, economic development, government policy, and public confidence.

We must do this while fusion power remains an uncertain eventuality. It is still too early to know whether fusion power will ever be able to compete economically with other forms of energy. The United States Department of Energy has estimated that the earliest a power-generating fusion reactor could operate is sometime after the year 2000. If such a reactor is successful, commercialization of the technology could come in the decade of the 2020s. In the meantime, we must define with greater clarity the role we want fission power to play in our energy future.

Renewable energy sources. Great uncertainties surround the future prospects of renewable energy resources. Technological advances are needed to further the development of virtually all renewable resources except hydroelectric power and passive solar architecture.

The growth in the use of any of these resources will depend largely on their cost. Perhaps hardest of all to predict is the possibility of a scientific breakthrough that will make possible the cheap and widespread use of one or more of these resources. Such a breakthrough could, for example, make photovoltaic cells much less expensive, vastly increasing their production and use. In any event, the contribution of all renewable resources to total U.S. energy needs is expected to remain well below 10 percent for the next several decades.

Future Energy Prospects

With this survey of future energy sources in mind, what can we say about our future energy prospects? In general, the possibilities for a stable energy future are strong as we approach the year 2000 and move into the twenty-first century. But many hard choices will have to be made and much hard work will be needed to achieve the goal of energy stability.

As for the longer-term future, the most thorough examination of the world's energy development, reaching into the twenty-first century, comes from the International Institute for Applied Systems Analysis (IIASA) in Austria.

The IIASA estimates that world population will double during the next half century, rising to about eight billion people. Providing energy for this many people will require increased use of all available fuels until we arrive at an era of "sustainable resources." IIASA predicts that will happen sometime in the late twenty-first century.

At that time, the world would have succeeded in creating a self-renewing supply of energy. This energy supply would be made possible by breeder reactors, solar power installations, and, perhaps, fusion energy machines. To make such an era possible will require building new energy production facilities at an enormous cost. The IIASA emphasizes the urgency of pointing toward this goal.

Our energy resources have been a cornerstone of civilization's progress. They have fueled mankind's long journey from the cave fires of Paleolithic man to today's rocket flights into space. Along the way, the ingenuity of the human mind has been able to devise the technological wonders, the Eiffel towers and offshore oil platforms, the computers and robots that astound and beguile us—and improve the quality of our lives.

We must assume that future technological wonders will come to pass. Consider in this light some of the energy proposals now on the drawing boards of scientists and planners at NASA, in think tanks, and in corporate research centers. One proposed space colony, for example, would process minerals from the moon using energy from the sun. Scientists from Princeton University and NASA suggest that such a colony might be built in a cylinder nineteen miles high and four miles in diameter. The cylinder would rotate every 114 seconds to simulate the pull of gravity. Inside, there would be a city of several million people.

Another NASA energy proposal is a free-flying solar power station which could be used to support the space shuttle on long-duration flights of up to 120 days. A third proposal, from Boeing Aerospace Company, would use solar heat to produce power in a space module. The sun's rays would be focused into a domelike structure by giant reflectors. Inside the structure a heated gas would be used to generate electricity.

Some of these projects may never come close to realization. But this kind of research and theorizing may well lead to scientific breakthroughs that will help to solve more earthbound energy problems.

As the long history of energy use suggests, when a need exists, there is a response to that need. In the future, as in the past, we must continue on the path of harnessing our planet's energy resources to meet the needs of mankind.

OVERLEAF: Near a city of the future, hydrogen-powered planes and solar-powered gliders fly above a motorway where electric cars have stopped to recharge. To the right, steam rises from a geothermal plant. At left, center, a robot machine cuts plants for fuel for the nearby power station. High voltage power lines carry electricity into the city and also support a monorail. In the city itself, the buildings are designed to make maximum use of solar energy. At upper left, a circle of microwave receivers get power from a solar satellite. In the distance (from left to right) are an oceanic power station, a string of wind propellers, and a coal mine and industrial plant.

Glossary

Acid Rain Rain, hail, or snow that has a high level of sulfuric or nitric acids. Some scientists believe that acid rain results mainly from the burning of coal and other fossil fuels in industrial and power plants.

Calorie A unit of heat energy. One calorie is the amount of heat needed to raise the temperature of 1 gram of water 1 degree Celsius. It is equivalent to 4.186 joules.

Electricity A form of energy that is generated as a current. Electricity is the result of the existence of electric charge. An object is said to be electrically charged if the number of its protons—positively charged particles—and the number of its electrons—negatively charged particles—are not equal.

Fission Energy Nuclear energy produced by splitting the heavy nucleus of an atom. In a nuclear reactor, fission of atoms of heavy elements, such as uranium, takes place, producing heat, which is then used to make steam to drive electric generators.

Fluidized Bed Combustion A process that burns crushed coal and limestone in a stream of air. Because this process removes sulfur pollutants as they form inside the combustion chamber, it reduces pollution.

Fossil Fuels Fuels formed from the decayed and compressed remains of ancient plants and sea animals. They include coal, petroleum, and natural gas.

Fuel Cell A disklike device in which a gaseous fuel is converted directly into electricity by means of a chemical reaction, without flame or pollution.

Fusion Energy Energy that results when nuclear particles fuse or join together. Current research aims at developing a fusion reactor.

Geothermal Energy Energy in the form of heat created in the interior of the earth. It is released in volcanic eruptions. Exploitable forms, such as hot springs, steam vents, and geysers may be harnessed to produce steam or hot water for generating electricity.

Hydrocarbons Organic compounds that contain only hydrogen and carbon. Petroleum consists primarily of numerous hydrocarbons.

Integrated Gasification Combined Cycle Plant A plant in which coal is transformed into a clean synthetic fuel before it is burned to generate electricity. A heat exchange between the two processes increases the efficiency of the operation.

Internal Combustion Engine An engine that burns liquid fuel in a chamber inside the engine. The explosion of the fuel creates an expanding gas that moves a piston. The piston's movement produces work, such as driving a car's wheels.

Joule A unit for measuring work and energy named after the British physicist James Joule.

Natural Gas A natural odorless fuel found in porous rocks, usually along with petroleum.

Nuclear Energy (Atomic Energy) The energy that is stored in the nucleus of an atom. It can be released through fission, fusion, or radioactive decay (see Fission Energy, Fusion Energy, Radioactivity).

Nuclear Reactor A device for producing nuclear energy through fission by a controlled nuclear chain reaction. One type of nuclear reactor, the breeder reactor, produces more nuclear fuel, in the form of plutonium, than it consumes (see Fission Energy).

Ocean-Thermal Energy Conversion A process in which warm surface waters and the colder ocean depths are used to heat and cool a liquid, usually ammonia, in order to generate electricity.

Oil Shale Porous sedimentary rock that contains a hydrocarbon called kerogen. The rock is heated to release kerogen, which is then refined into synthetic fuel.

Photosynthesis The process by which green plants manufacture carbohydrates. In the process, chlorophyll converts light energy into a sugar, glucose.

Radioactivity A form of nuclear energy that occurs when the nucleus of an atom decays or disintegrates spontaneously and emits particles and/or electromagnetic waves. Radium and uranium both exhibit natural radiation. Other elements disintegrate or decay if they are bombarded with high-energy particles.

Solar Cell (Photovoltaic Cell) A device, generally made of layers of silicon, that converts the sun's energy into electricity.

Solar Energy Energy radiated by the sun, including heat, light, radio waves, and X-rays. The sun's energy can be used directly for heating or it can be converted into electricity by devices such as the solar cell.

Steam Engine An engine in which water is heated to produce steam. The expanding steam passes through a valve into a cylinder, where it pushes a piston.

Synthetic Fuels Liquid and gaseous fuels usually manufactured from coal, oil shale, and tar sands.

Tar Sands Sands that contain a very heavy, black sticky hydrocarbon called bitumen. The sands are heated to release the bitumen, which is then refined into synthetic fuel.

Thermodynamics The science concerned with the nature of heat and how it is converted into other forms of energy, such as mechanical energy.

Tidal Energy Energy produced by the daily rise and fall of the tides. It can be used to drive turbines for generating electricity.

Tokamak A machine used in research on the development of a fusion energy reactor. It creates powerful magnetic fields that confine heavy hydrogen nuclei in order to produce fusion (see Fusion Energy).

Turbine A rotary engine with a series of blades attached to a central rotating wheel. It may be powered by the force of water, steam, or hot gases. A wind turbine is a giant wind machine with propeller-type blades that converts wind energy into electrical energy.

Index

Boldface numbers indicate illustrations.

Acid Rain, 76–77
AEC (Atomic Energy Commission), 85
Agriculture, 15, 36, 52
American Revolutionary War, 43
Animal power, 36–37, 45: horses, 46, 52–53; oxen, 37, **37**
Annapolis Basin Tidal Power Project, 98–99, **98–99**, 101
Ashland Oil Company, 71
Athabasca, Alberta, Canada, 63, 71, 72
Atomic energy, 81–83
Atoms for Peace Plan, 84
Automobiles, 10, 35, 51–55, 65, 68:— pollution, 68

Babylonians, 36–37
Barstow, CA, 4, **4**, 76, 94
Beaufort Sea, AK, 61
Beaumont, TX, 55
Bell, Alexander Graham, 48
Benz, Karl, 53
Bern, Switzerland, 80
Bessemer steel producing process, 46–48, **46**
Bicycles, 23
Bitumen, 71–73
Boeing Aerospace Company, 107
Boston, MA, 48
Breeder reactors, 21, 87, **87**
Brickmaking, 41
British Gas Corporation, 68
BTU (British Thermal Unit), 30, 33
Burton, William M., 55

Cadillac Automobile Company, 54
California, 4, 46, 76, 88, 94, 96, 99
Caloric heat, 29
Canada, 7, 63, 71–73, 98–99, 101
Carnot, Nicolas, 31
Catlettsburg, KY, 71
Centennial Exposition, Philadelphia, 1876, 24
Chicago, IL, 10, 48, 52–53
Chief Joseph Dam, WA, 91, **91**
Coal, 10, 13, 15, 18, 23, 33, 43–47, 67–76 passim, 89, 91, 105–6: gas from, 68;—mining, 13, 41–47, **42**, **47**, 67–69, 107, **107**; oil from, 70; reserves, 24, **24**; varieties of, 67–68
Coal oil, 55, 57, 70, 73
Colorado, 73
Columbia River, 92
Columbia University, New York City, 81
Computerization, 15, 22, 65, **65**
Conservation, 15, 64
Consolidated Edison Company, NY, 76
Cotton, 43

Daimler, Gottlieb, 53
Dams, 91, **91**, 92. See Hydroelectric power.
Darrieus, G. J. M., 97
Deep-sea oil drilling, 21, 23–24
Diesel fuel, 56, 68
Drake, Edwin L., 55, **55**, 57

Dunning, John R., 81, **81**
Duquesne Light Company, 85
Duryea Brothers, Charles and Frank, 53

Ecology. See Environmental effects.
Edison, Thomas Alva, 48–49, **49**
EDS (Exxon Donor Solvent), 70
Egyptians, 39, 64
Eiffel Tower, Paris, France, 103, 107
Einstein, Albert, 29, 80, **80**, 81, 95
Eisenhower, Pres. Dwight D., 84
Electric Power Research Institute, Palo Alto, CA, 86, 106
Electricity, 7–17 passim, 21–23, 28, **28**, 32–33, 49, 52–53, 67, 85–95 passim, 98, 105, 107
Engines: gasoline, 32; internal combustion, 30, **30**, 39, 51, 54, **54**; steam, 30, **30**, 31–32, 35, 41–45; turbine jet, 30, **30**, 31–32
England, 40–48 passim, 59
Environmental effects, 37, 69, 92. See also Pollution.
Environmental Protection Agency, 77
EPCOT Center, 14, **14**, 17–24, **20–24**
Evans, Oliver, 39
Exxon Corporation, 17–24, **17–24**, 70, 73

Faraday, Michael, 29, 32–33
Fermi, Enrico, 79–82, **81**, 84
Fire, 18, 35–36
Fission, 10, 81–83, 87–88
Flatiron Building, NY, 48, **48**
Fluidized bed combustion, 10, 74, **74**. See Coal.
Food chain, 18, 27
Ford, Henry, 51–56 passim
Ford, Model-A, 52, **52**
Ford, Model-T, 54, 56
FPC (Federal Power Commission), 66
France, 21, 43, 87, 93, **93**, 103, 106
Frisch, Otto, 82
Fuel, 18, 23–24, 29, 35–48, 65: coal, 18, 40–45, 65; crude oil, 55; diesel, 68; fossil fuels, 14–15, 18, 20–21, 29, 39, 65–68, 76–77, 91; gasoline, 55, 68; kerosene, 55; natural gas, 18, 36, 45, 65–66; nuclear, 14, **14**; petroleum, 54–57; synthetic, 65, 72–73; whale oil, 45, 47; wood, 35–41, 45–46, 99, 101
Fuel cell, 8, 76, **76**
Fulton, Robert, 42
Fundy, Bay of, 7, 98, 100–1
Furth, Harold, 89, **89**
Fusion, 10, 15, 21, 79, **79**, 87–89, **89**, 106

Gas: coal —, 68; LNG, 67; methane, 58, 68; natural —, 13, 18, 36, 45, 65–67; synthetic, 10. See also Petroleum.
Gasoline, 29, 55, 63. See Petroleum.
Geothermal energy, 11, **11**, 15, 39, 89, 91, 98–101, **100**, 107
Gesner, Abraham, 70
Geysers, The, CA, 11, **11**. See Geothermal energy.
Gilbert, William, 32

Glasgow University, Scotland, 41
Goldendale, WA, 96
Great Canadian Oil Sands, Ltd., 72
"Greenhouse effect," 77. See Pollution and Environmental effects.

Hahn, Otto, 81
Heat, 30–31, 33: caloric —, 29
Heating/Cooling systems, 30–33, 65, 92. See also Solar energy.
Henry, Joseph, 31–33, **31**
Hitler, Adolf, 81
Humphreys, Robert E., 55
Huntsville, AL, 93
Hydrocarbon Research, Inc., 71
Hydroelectric power, 27, 48, 65, 91, **91**, 92, 101

IBG (Intermediate BTU Gas), 68
Iceland, 100
IGCC (Integrated Gasification Combined Cycle), 74, 76
IIASA (International Institute for Applied Systems Analysis), Austria, 107
India, 99
Indians of North America, 39, 67, 72–73
Industrial Revolution, 18, 35, **35**, 38, 42, 48, 51, 77
Inertial confinement, 88. See Fusion.
Institute of Nuclear Power Operations, Atlanta, GA, 86
Iran, 64
Israel, 64

Japan, 83
Jersey Central Power and Light Company, Oyster Creek, NJ, 85
Joule, James, 30

KWh (kilowatt hours), 33, 35, 49
Kaiser Wilhelm Institute, Berlin, 81
Kerogen, 71, 73, **73**
Kerosene, 55, 57, 70, 73. See Fuel.
Kuwait, 63

Lawrence Livermore National Laboratory, San Francisco, CA, 88
Lexington, KY, 52
LMFBR (Liquid metal fast breeder reactor), 87
LNG (Liquified natural gas), 67, **67**
Los Alamos, NM, 83
Lurgi process, 68, 74
LWR (Light water reactor), 84–85, 87, 106

Maglev (magnetically levitated trains), 8
Magnetic confinement, 88. See Fusion.
Magnetism, 29, 33
Maine, 7
Manhattan Project, 82. See Atomic energy.
Mass production, 51
Medicine Bow, WY, 96
Meitner, Lise, 81–82
Mesopotamians, 36

Metallurgy, 41
Methane. *See* Gas.
Metropolitan Edison Company, Harrisburg, PA, 85. *See* Three Mile Island Nuclear Power Station.
MFTF-B (Mirror Fusion Test Facility B), 88. *See* Fusion.
Middle East, 36–39: oil reserves, 67
Milan, OH, 49
Mining: iron ore, 43. *See also* Coal.
Mitchell, Dana P., 81, **81**
Morse, Samuel F. B., 48

Natural gas, 18, 105. *See also* LNG *and* Methane.
National Academy of Sciences, 77
USS *Nautilus,* 84
New Brunswick, N.S., Canada, 7
New Oil Field, The (1882), 57, **57**
New York City, 8, 35, **35,** 48–49, **49**
New York *Herald,* 49
Newcomen, Thomas, 41
North Sea, 7, 21, 59, **59,** 61, 103–4. *See* Oil, offshore drilling.
NOVA laser, 88
NSAC (Nuclear Safety Analysis Center), Palo Alto, CA, 86
Nuclear Non-Proliferation Treaty, 84
Nuclear power, 10, 13–14, 65, 74, 77, 82, **82,** 84–89, 106
Nuclear reactor, 11, 83, **83:** core, 24, 33
Nuclear Regulatory Commission, 85
Nuclear submarines, 84

Oak Ridge National Laboratory, Oak Ridge, TN, 82, 84
Occidental Petroleum Company, 73
OECD (Organization for Economic Cooperation and Development), 77
Offshore oil drilling. *See* Oil.
Oil, 13, 18, 21–24, 36, 39, 51–67 passim, 89, 92: for cooking, 37, **37;** crude —, 55, 63, 70–71; deep-sea drilling for, 21, 23–24; fuel, 4, **4,** 60; heating, 23–24, **24,** 60, 65, 71–72; lighting, 45, 57; offshore drilling, 4, 7, **7,** 21– 24, **22,** 58–59, **58–59,** 103–7; refineries, 10, 51; Spindletop Field gusher, 53, **53,** 55; synthetic, 70–71, 105
Oil shale, 23–24, **24,** 65, 71–73, **73**
Olds Automobile Company, 54
Oldsmobile, 54
OTEC (Ocean-thermal energy conversion), 12–13, **13,** 101, 107, **107**
Otto, Nikolaus, 53

Paducah, KY, 74
Passamaquoddy Bay, 100–1
Pacific Gas & Electric Company, 96, 98
Petroleum, 13, 15, 37, 51, 56–65 passim, 70–76 passim, 104–5

Phénix, 21. *See* Breeder reactors.
Photosynthesis, 18, 27, 29
Piceance Basin, CO, 73
Pig iron, 47–48
Pittsburgh, PA, 47, **47**
Plutonium, 86–87; —fuel, 87
Pollution, 13, 15, 35, 68, 73–76, **74,** 99
Princeton Plasma Physics Laboratory, Princeton, NJ, 88–89, 107
Printing, 41
Prometheus, 36, **36**
Prudhoe Bay, Alaska, 58–60

Radioactive waste, 86–87. *See* Pollution.
Railroads, 8, 45–46, 51, 56
Rance River, Brittany, France, 100
Richmond, VA, 67
Rickover, Adm. Hyman G., 84
Robotics, 15, 33, **33,** 107, **107**
Rockefeller, John D., 57
Roman Empire, 38, 39
Rutherford, Ernest, 80

Sacramento Municipal Utility District, CA, 96
Sailing vessels, 38–39, **38,** 41. *See also* Wind power.
Sandia Laboratories, Albuquerque, NM, 97
Satellites, 4, **4,** 21
Saudi Arabia, 21, 60, **60,** 63–64
Savery, Thomas, 41
Shippingport Atomic Power Station, Pittsburgh, PA, 85
SHIVA laser, 88
Skyscrapers, 48, 69
SNG (Substitute natural gas), 70
Solano County, CA, 96
Solar energy, 11, 15, 17, 21–28, **25–28,** 39, 65, 89–95, 101–3, **103,** 106–7, **106–7:** electricity from, 4, **4,** 8, 94–95, **94,** 107; for heating, 92–94, **93;** satellites, 11, 101; Solar One, 95
South Africa, 70
Southern California Edison Company, 76, 95–96, 99: —Cool Water Power Plant, 76; —Geothermal Power Plant, 99
Soviet Union, 63, 67
Stagecoach, 46
Standard Oil Company, 57
Stanley Steamer, 52
Stagg Field, University of Chicago, 10, 79, 82
Statfjord B oil drilling platform, 103
Steam power, 11, 18, 41–43, **42, 43,** 52, 100
Stephenson, George, 44
Stephenson Rocket, 44, **44**
Strassman, Fritz, 81

Strathcona Oil Refinery, Edmonton, Alberta, Canada, 51, **51**
Syncrude Canada, Ltd., 71–72, **71**
Szilard, Leo, 81–82

Tar sands, 21, 63, **63,** 65, 71–72, **71**
Tennessee Valley Authority, 74
Textiles industry, 41–42, 45–46
TFTR (Tokamak Fusion Test Reactor), 88–89, **89.** *See* Fusion.
Thermodynamics, 29, 31
Thompson, Benjamin (Count Rumford), 29–30
Three Mile Island, PA, 11, 84–86, **86.** *See* Nuclear Reactor.
Tidal energy, 7, 98–99. *See* Annapolis project.
Titusville, PA, 55, **55,** 57
Tokamak (toroidal magnetic chamber), 21, 88. *See* Glossary.
Trade, 39–41
Trans-Alaska Pipeline, 21, 59–61, **60**
Trevithick, Richard, 42
Truman, Pres. Harry S, 83
Turbines, 11: steam —, 74, 95; jet, 30–32, **30.** *See* Engines.

Union Oil Company of California, 73, 99
United Nations, 84
U.S. Bureau of Mines, 73
U.S. Department of Energy, 88
Universe of Energy, EPCOT Center, FL, 17–24, **17–22**
Uranium, 11, 14, **14,** 79, 82–91 passim

Valdez, Prince William Sound, AK, 21, 59–60
Vehicles: battery-operated, 22, 33; diesel-run, 56; electrically powered, 21–22, 52–53. *See* Engines.
Von Guericke, Otto, 32
Von Helmholz, Hermann, 30–31
Von Helmont, Jan, 68

Washington, George, 45
Watt, James 41–43, **43**
Water power, 28, **28,** 40, **40,** 91–92, 100–1, 105, 107
Water wheels, 38–39, 42
Westinghouse, George, 49
Whaling, 45, **45,** 57: for oil, 45
Wind power, 11, 15, 38–39, 89, 91, 96, 107, **107**
Windmills, 21, 38–39, **38,** 96–97, **96**
Wood, 35–46, 99–101, **101:** for electricity, 101; shortage of, 39–41, 77
World Coal Study, 67, 105
World War II, 66–68, 70, 73, 82
World's Columbian Exposition, Chicago, 1893, 24